callaloo, calypso & carnival

the cuisines of trinidad and tobago

Books by Dave DeWitt

The Food Lover's Handbook to the Southwest

Texas Monthly Guide to New Mexico

Pepper Gardening (with Paul Bosland)

The Fiery Cuisines (with Nancy Gerlach)

Fiery Appetizers (with Nancy Gerlach)

The Whole Chile Pepper Book (with Nancy Gerlach)

Hot Spots Just North of the Border (with Nancy Gerlach)

Callaloo, Calypso & Carnival

the cuisines of trinidad and tobago

by
dave dewitt &
Mary jane Wilan

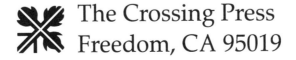
The Crossing Press
Freedom, CA 95019

Acknowledgements

Thanks to the following people who helped to make this book a reality: Mary Angai, Mary Jane and Robert Barnes, Joe brown, Michael and Danielle Coelho, Diana Cohen-Chan, Roy Edwards, Ramesh Ghany, Dennis Hayes, Irvine Jackson, Brian Kuei Tung, Duffy and Kimoy Lamy, Martin Lawrence, Ellie Leavitt, Steve Mathura, Vernon and Irene Montrichard, Johnny Nahous, Keith Nexar, marie Perementer, Reginald and Basil Phillips, mikey and Nancy Ramesar, and Keith Toby.

Library of Congress Cataloging-in-Publication Data

DeWitt, Dave
    Callaloo, Calypso, and carnival: the cuisine of Trinidad and Tobago / by Dave DeWitt and Mary Jane Wilan.
        p.   cm.
    Includes index.
    ISBN 0-89594-639-4. — ISBN 0-89594-638-6 (pbk.)
    1. Cookery, Trinidadian.   2. Trinidad and Tobago—Description and travel.
I. Wilan, Mary Jane. II. Title
TX716. T7D49   1993
641.5972983—dc20
                                            93-21671
                                          CIP

For Marie Permenter and
Vernon and Irene Montrichard,
with thanks.

Contents

Introduction

Our fascination with Trinidad and Tobago goes back to 1976, when Dave was mesmerized by a group of musicians with the name Trinidad and Tobago National Steel Drum Band, which performed at the Texas State Fair in Dallas. Back in those days, Dave was peddling loofah sponges at that fair to pay for his writing habit, which had yet to flourish, but that's ancient history. Part of the entertainment during lunch break at the fair was the steel drum band, and Dave was amazed by the range of sounds emanating from the sawed-off, fifty-five-gallon steel drums. It sounded like a full orchestra. When the band took a break, Dave went up on stage to look for the concealed electric guitars, but of course there weren't any. After listening to the band perform every day for weeks, Dave vowed that some day he would visit Trinidad and Tobago.

Sixteen years later, we were touring the steel drum practice yards in Port of Spain, and it was all Dennis Hayes' doing. Marketing director of The Crossing Press, he had casually mentioned to us that he was trying to find writers for a book on the food and music of Trinidad and Tobago. We jumped at the chance—not only for the challenge and the opportunity to go "down de islands," but also because we had friends in Port of Spain who were in the food business—a perfect combination!

Several years earlier, we had met Marie Permenter and Irene Montrichard at the National Fiery Foods Show in Albuquerque. They were exhibiting their Trinidad Pepper Sauce, which they manufacture in Trindad and distribute from Florida with Mary Jane and Robert Barnes (Marie's daughter and son-in-law). Marie and Irene invited us to visit them in Trinidad, but at that time we were unable to go. Years later, when we faxed Marie about the Trinidad and Tobago (T&T) book project, she volunteered to assist us by planning nearly every moment of our lives for two solid weeks. A flood of faxes from Port of Spain with appointments and schedules proved that we were headed to paradise to work, not to party. Or so we thought.

Our visit to Trinidad began with a dinner party at the home that Marie Permenter shares with Vernon and Irene Montrichard. These three entrepreneurs founded the Royal Castle chain of spicy chicken and chips restaurants in 1968, then fought off the incursion of Kentucky Fried Chicken, and are currently setting sales records at thirteen locations in Trinidad and Tobago (see Chapter 3).

At the party at their home overlooking a lovely bay, we met the cast of characters whom Marie and Vernon had lined up to be our culinary guides. Mikey and Nancy Ramesar gave us lessons on East Indian cooking West Indian style. Keith Nexar and Steve Mathura, directors of AdVantage, the advertising agency responsible for much of Royal Castle's success, set up our interviews with chefs and even arranged for our appearance on local television. Michael Coelho, marketing director of the Royal Castle chain, was our main guide and drove us all over Trinidad. Because of the efforts of these people, we were able to complete our research and fall in love with the country at the same time.

The Republic of Trinidad and Tobago is often called simply Trinidad, which is incorrect. To avoid confusion, when referring to the country, we use the common island abbreviation T&T. When referring to the separate islands rather than the country, we use either Trinidad or Tobago. The terms "Trinidadian" and "Trini" seem to be acceptable for describing the people of both islands.

A word about the food. It was impossible to include every single T&T recipe we encountered. Rather, we have selected those that we consider to be the tastiest and most representative of the multi-faceted cuisine, and we have combined them with recent innovations from T&T chefs and a few of our own T&T-influenced creations.

Although this book was not designed to be a travel guide, we were so taken by the attractions of T&T that we have included a brief initial chapter to describe the travel highlights for visitors. Also, in the Appendix, we have provided specific resources for travelers. Other resources provided at the back of this book include mail order sources, a glossary of Trini terms, a bibliography, and a discography—a list of our favorite calypso, steel-band, and *soca* recordings. The best travel guide to T&T is the Insight Guide called simply *Trinidad and Tobago*.

Before delving into the culture of T&T, we should inform readers about Congo chile peppers. They are the T&T pod type of *Capsicum chinense*, which has the hottest peppers of any species, but they are not available outside of T&T, except from hobbyist gardeners like ourselves, who have Congo pepper seeds. (Please don't call us for them—we barely have enough for ourselves!) The most similar hot chile peppers available in the United States are Mexican Habaneros, now being grown in California, Texas, and Florida, and imported Scotch bonnets from Jamaica. Habaneros and Scotch bonnets are extremely hot and should be used with caution; cooks should wear rubber gloves when handling them.

In nearly every case, Congo peppers can be replaced with a hot sauce from Chapter 4 or a commercial Habanero hot sauce. Mail order sources for these peppers and Trinidadian hot sauces are included in the Appendix. Frieda's by Mail in Los Angeles sells dried Habaneros year-round and fresh Habaneros in season. Other fresh hot chile peppers such as jalapeños and serranos may be substituted, but the flavor will not be the same.

So put on some calypso or *soca* music, mix a favorite rum drink from Chapter 5, grab your hot chile peppers, and head for the kitchen. You're about to experience the most unique country and cuisine in all of the Caribbean!

Liming about:
enjoying t&t

"Two unspoiled islands, one country—Trinidad and Tobago," pronounced Brian Kuei Tung, Minister of Trade, Industry and Tourism. We were sitting in his spacious high-rise office, overlooking the Port of Spain harbor, and the minister was telling us how different his country was from other places called paradise.

"We don't allow logging, so the rain forests are intact," he said. "And we don't allow high-rise hotels to spoil our beaches."

We were amazed. A country that actually was protecting its scenic beauty and not caving in to big business and developers? Hard to believe, but apparently true. As we drove around the two islands, we found nothing to contradict the minister's description of his country. Consider Trinidad: About the size of Rhode Island, it has maxi-taxis, rain forests, and a lake of pitch. Consider Tobago: About the size of Martha's Vineyard, it has lovely beaches, a magical reef, and a mystery tombstone. "Trinidad is for travelers," the minister also told us, "Tobago is for tourists." However, both are perfect for liming.

To "lime," according to a local dictionary of Trini slang, is "to pass the time in idle pleasure." It describes every possible form of indulgence except Carnival, which is more of a frantic adventure than an idle pleasure. Liming is hangin' out, goofin' off, fishin', drivin', swimmin', boatin', picnickin', and generally just doing anything one wants to do. For us, to lime was to explore the land, the people, and the food of Trinidad and Tobago.

Port of Spain

Most visitors to T&T fly into Trinidad and land at Piarco International Airport, which sits in the middle of rice fields southeast of Port of Spain. The city is an easy drive from the airport on a divided highway, passing many roadside vendors selling everything from coconuts to "doubles." Half of the 1.3 million people in T&T live along this east-west corridor, from Chaguaramas in the west to Arima in the north center of the island. And half of these people live in Port of Spain, which has grown from a small fishing village in 1757 to the urban sprawl we see today. The growth has overtaken towns that are now absorbed into the metropolitan area but still maintain their identity as suburbs: St. James, Maraval, Laventille, St. Clair, St. Ann's, and others. Most of the population lives in these suburbs, but the downtown part of the city is filled during the day with government workers, shop owners, and shoppers.

The downtown section of Port of Spain is a wild medley of historic buildings, ramshackle shops, modern high-rise buildings, street vendors camped on the sidewalks, and seemingly thousands of maxi-taxis—vans that serve as the main method of public transportation.

Independence Square, near the harbor, is the focal point of the downtown area and was reclaimed from swampland in 1816. Today it is surrounded by government buildings, such as the Financial Complex, with its twin, twenty-two-story towers. We ate several delicious meals at Johnny's Food Haven, which serves native, or Creole, food. Other downtown attractions include Frederick Street, the main shopping street; Woodford Square on Frederick Street, which is a lovely park that serves as a public forum for all kinds of people; the Red House, the seat of Parliament, which overlooks Woodford Square and has Chambers that are open to the public; and the National Museum and Art Gallery, at Frederick and Keane streets, with a collection of paintings by Cazabon, Trinidad's most noted nineteenth-century artist.

The most dramatic section of Port of Spain is the Queen's Park Savannah, a 232-acre park that is three miles in circumference. This vast area is the site of the Trinidad Turf Club, a racetrack with three racing seasons each year. It's fun to see the thoroughbreds exercising in the morning amidst grazing egrets and to watch soccer clubs practicing in the afternoon. On the streets surrounding the Savannah are the usual collection of vendors selling coconut water, jelly nuts, barbecued chicken, corn on the cob, and sweets.

On the northern edge of the Savannah are the zoo and the botanic gardens. The Emperor Valley Zoo, which opened in 1952, has an extensive collection of T&T wildlife and is probably the best zoo in the Caribbean. The Botanic Gardens, the oldest in the Western Hemisphere, were laid out in 1820 and contain not only the official residences of the president and prime minister, but also the graves of many of the early governors. The gardens were described by F. A. Ober, author of *The Knockabout Club in the West Indies*, in 1888: "Its [Port of Spain's] chief attraction is the great botanic gardens in the suburbs, where are gathered all the vegetable wonders of the Spice Islands: palms in every variety, bamboos in feathery clumps, and flowering plants of every kind." His description is still true today; parrots fly through the tall trees, ferns abound, and there are such botanical oddities as "Napoleon's Hat" and a tree called "Raw Beef" because of the red color of its sap.

On the western side of the Savannah is a collection of historic colonial mansions called "The Magnificent Seven." Although the buildings are in varying degrees of renovation and are not open to the public, it's fun to walk by them and admire "Killarney," a scaled-down version of Balmoral Castle in Scotland; "Whitehall," a Venetian-style mansion; and five other striking buildings, including the German Renaissance-style Queen's Royal College, attended by T&T's famed novelist V. S. Naipaul.

Lodging in Port of Spain ranges from quaint guesthouses to the 400-room Trinidad Hilton, which has the distinction of being the only upside-down hotel in the world. Since it is built on a steep slope, guests enter the lobby at the top of the hotel and descend to their rooms. Incidentally, once a week the Hilton holds a Carnival Theme Night, which offers Creole food and an interesting cultural show featuring calypso music. It's an entertaining introduction to T&T culture; we were surprised to remember lyrics to calypso songs that our parents listened to in the fifties.

We stayed at the Kapok Hotel, a small (seventy-one-room) establishment adjacent to the northwest corner of the Savannah. It was friendly and convenient not only to the Savannah but also to the shops along Saddle Road in Maraval. Other recommended hotels include the Hotel Normandie in St. Ann's with its lovely shops, the Chaconia Inn in Maraval, the Valley Vue in St. Ann's, the Queen's Park Hotel on the edge of the Savannah, and, of course, the Holiday Inn downtown.

Dining in Port of Spain and the surrounding towns is nothing short of heaven, since T&T has the most diverse cuisine in the Caribbean. Because of the numerous ethnic influences on the country's food (see Chapter 3), it is a visitor's duty to sample as many of the delights as possible. We don't have space here to give extensive restaurant listings, but following are a few recommendations—assuming,

of course, that the establishments are still in business. You might call them before going. Many of these restaurants gave us recipes, which appear in Chapters 4 through 10. For native or Creole food, try The Breakfast Shack, Johnny's Food Haven, The Verandah in St. Clair, Rafters on Warner Street in Newtown, and the Veni Mange in St. James. For East Indian specialties, the Patraj Roti Shop in San Juan and Monsoon on Tragarete Road are recommended. We didn't dine at very many Chinese restaurants, but the Tiki Village at the Kapok Hotel is highly recommended. We visited two excellent restaurants that served a combination of innovative Caribbean seafood and international dishes: the Solimar in St. Ann's and the Cafe Savannah at the Kapok. Both were superb. For Lebanese food, the Ali Baba in Maraval is good. These are not the only fine restaurants in Port of Spain, but they're a great place to start dining.

Shopping is too easy in Port of Spain. Not only is there downtown Frederick Street with its bazaarlike conglomeration of shops, vendors, and food markets, there are also numerous shopping malls and plazas. Recommended shopping centers are Long Circular Mall in St. James, West Mall in Westmoorings, Royal Palm Plaza in Maraval, and the Galleria Shopping Complex in St. James. Although T&T is not renowned for its handicrafts, there are some beautiful examples of batik, wood carvings, and copper crafts that can be purchased. Other favorite island items include Trini rums, fine art, tropical T-shirts and other clothing, and CDs of calypso, soca, and steel-band music.

Off the beaten tourist path, but of great interest to food lovers, is the Central Market on Beetham Highway, just east of downtown. This sprawling complex contains literally every food item available in T&T, from gigantic pumpkins to salt cod to Indian masala spices to dasheen (taro) leaves. Our guide to the market was Johnny Nahous, owner of Johnny's Food Haven. He was shopping for produce for his restaurant and took us along for a tour of the bustling market—where, if you're not careful, you can get run over by a barrow full of cabbages. Vendors raised their prices when they saw the foreigners with him, but Johnny waved them off in disgust and pursued the bargains. The massive piles of Congo chile peppers were particularly impressive.

Port of Spain is a convenient jumping-off point for an exploration of the rest of the country. Tobago is twelve minutes away by air, and since the farthest point on Trinidad is only a three-hour drive, day trips from the capital are easy and fun.

Trinidad Sight-Seeing

Port of Spain sits at the foot of the Northern Range of mountains, so there are spectacular views of the city from the surrounding hills, especially from Fort George in the western part of the city, from Lady Young Road on the way to San Juan, and from the narrow, winding Lady Chancellor Road just off the Savannah.

To the west of Port of Spain is Chaguaramas, a former U.S. military base, which now is the yachting center of Trinidad. There are numerous marinas here, and the area is known throughout the Caribbean as a relatively inexpensive location for yacht renovation. Chaguaramas is also the point of embarcation for going "down de islands," or sailing to the outlying resort islands such as Gasparee, with its Fantasy Island Resort. This group of offshore islands is also renowned for its fine fishing.

One of the most popular trips from Port of Spain is to Maracas Bay, about thirty-five minutes away on the North Shore. En route, along the North Coast Road, are spectacular views of the coast and off-shore islands. At the designated lookouts, calypsonians will compose and sing personalized calypsos for visitors for a small fee. Maracas Bay is a medium-sized, protected beach with numerous shark-and-bake shacks selling this favorite seafood snack. The locals will gleefully inform you that the boats out in the bay are fishing for sharks! Fortunately, the sharks don't enter the shallow water near the shore. Less than a mile from the road is the Maracas Waterfall, which plunges about a hundred yards.

Farther east along the North Coast is the tiny village of Blanchisseuse, where the Marianne River flows into the surf, and the rain forests tower above. It is one of the most beautiful places we have ever visited. Fortunately, the chances of Blanchisseuse being spoiled by high-rise hotels with discos and casinos is practically nil.

From Blanchisseuse, there is a marvelous road through the Northern Range that eventually ends up at Arima. It is remarkable to be able to drive through so many square miles of pristine rain forest, with some trees that are more than 150 feet tall. The rain forest is home to a large variety of wildlife. There are more than 400 species of birds in T&T (including 19 species of hummingbirds), 622 species of butterflies, and 700 species of orchids. Most of them are found in the Northern Range. The mammals include ocelots, *quenks* (peccaries), *manicous* (opossums), nine-banded armadillos, and brocket deer. Hopefully, the visitor won't run into a fer-de-lance or a bushmaster, two extremely dangerous vipers of the Northern Range. We did not encounter any, but then again, we never wandered far into the jungle.

Bird-watching is one of the main tourist attractions of the Northern Range, and the headquarters for this pastime is the 193-acre Asa Wright Nature Centre and Lodge, in the cool mountains north of Arima. Located at an altitude of about 3,000 feet, the center has a waterfall pool for cooling off, a twenty-three-room biology camp, and a plantation Great House with twenty-foot ceilings. Researchers stay at the camp; bird watchers live in colonial comfort at the Great House. The center was formerly a cocoa, coffee, and citrus plantation. Nearby, via a jungle trail, is Dunston Cave, the home of the world's most accessible colony of nocturnal oilbirds. These extremely rare, night-flying birds feed on fruit they grab in flight from trees.

Birds are also the main attraction of the Caroni Swamp, which sprawls just south of Port of Spain. Fifteen thousand acres of marshland, tidal lagoons, and mangrove trees, the swamp is a primary roosting ground for thousands of scarlet ibises. They are spectacularly colorful when in flight near sunset; it's no wonder that they are one of two national birds of T&T (the other is the cocrico, a tropical pheasant indigenous to Tobago). There are boat tours of Caroni swamp available, but watch out for twenty-foot-long anacondas, snakes that are so large they can swallow six-foot caimans—or you, for that matter—whole.

Incidentally, one of the most famous fishes swimming in T&T's swamps is called "millions" by Trinis because of its procreative proclivities. During the early part of this century they were fished extensively for the aquarium trade, where they became known as guppies, after Lechmere Guppy, T&T's most famous nineteenth-century ichthyologist.

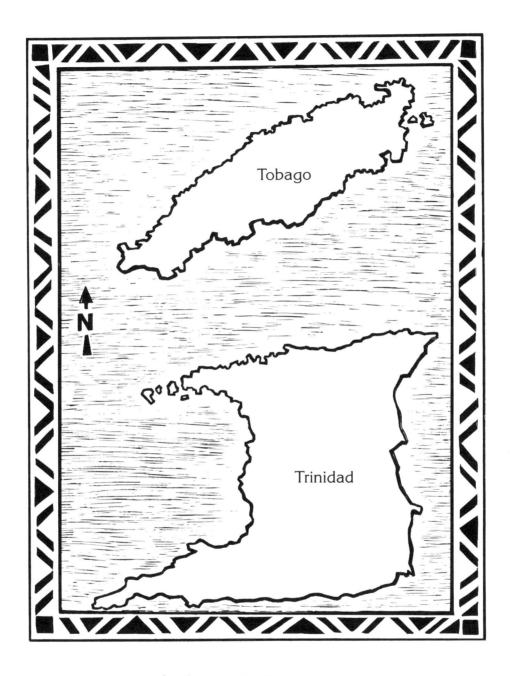

Tobago

Trinidad

trinidad & tobago

Another nature-oriented attraction is turtle watching at Matura Bay on the east coast. Strictly supervised by the government, the beach at Matura is the March through June nesting ground of the 500-pound leatherback turtles. The T&T Field Naturalists' Club and some private companies conduct tours during the turtles' nesting season.

The southern two-thirds of Trinidad has fewer tourist attractions than the northern part and is not as well traveled. It is a land of coconut groves, sugarcane fields, rolling savannahs, and heavy industry, such as oil refineries. However, there are some beautiful nearly deserted beaches, such as Mayaro and Manzanilla on the east coast.

One of the most intriguing sights in the southern part of the island is La Brea Pitch Lake, about forty-eight miles south of Port of Spain at the miniscule village of La Brea. Locally referred to as the eighth wonder of the world, this 115-acre lake of gunk contains the largest known deposits of natural asphalt in the world. A person can walk on the surface but had better not stand in one place for very long. In addition to being a natural resource, Pitch Lake is a symbol of the petroleum reserves of the country.

A small local museum traces the lake's colorful history, such as Sir Walter Raleigh using the lake's pitch to caulk his ships in 1595. The viewing gallery overlooks the 135-foot-deep lake as it is mined by heavy machinery. The lake miraculously replenishes itself from a fault line in the sandstone 250 feet below. Mastodon teeth and other fossils have been recovered from the pitch, giving us a hint of the early fauna of the island. In Barbados, chocolate cakes and puddings are named in honor of this geological wonder; curiously, we found no such named Trinidadian desserts.

Laid-Back Tobago

In many ways, it's easier to lime in Tobago than Trinidad. The difference between the two islands was pointed out by one of our Tobagonian guides, Basil Phillips. He told us, "Everyt'ing runs slower in Tobago."

Although the two islands are united politically and are separated by only twenty-one miles of sea, there is a world of difference between them. Trinidad is business oriented; Tobago is tourist oriented. Many residents of Trinidad escape to Tobago just to

lime and get away from it all. But just because Tobago is one-sixteenth the size of Trinidad doesn't mean there's nothing to see. As one travel guide noted, "A drive across the island discloses an abundance of hidden coves, eccentric villages, wild and deserted beaches."

Tobago is more of a typical Caribbean island than Trinidad because it is out of the path of Venezuela's Orinoco River, which prevents coral growth around Trinidad and clouds the water. Tobagonian waters, by contrast, are crystal clear and dotted with coral formations that attract scuba divers and snorkelers. The primary underwater attraction is Buccoo Reef, off the extreme western tip of the island. The jumping-off point to explore the reef is Store Bay, a small village with a pleasant beach. From here the visitor can hire a "glass-bottomed" boat (most are not glass but Plexiglas) for a trip to see the underwater wonders. The boatmen provide snorkeling gear, but dedicated snorkelers should bring their own.

About halfway out to the reef is the Nylon Pool, which features warm, shallow water over a sand bar, which is delightful for swimming. There are beautiful coral formations and fish (French angels, grunts, and butterfly fish), although the reef is greatly endangered by boats and anchors, which have destroyed most of the coral heads. For more adventurous divers, there are dive instructors and guides who can direct scuba enthusiasts to the less-frequented reefs, such as those along the northeast coast of Tobago.

Other places of interest on the western end of Tobago include Pigeon Point, a lovely, private beach with a small entrance fee; Bon Accord Lagoon, which is good for shell collecting; Crown Point, with a nearby cave that locals claim inspired the story of Robinson Crusoe; and Great Courland Bay, where loggerhead turtles come to nest in the spring. Scattered along the beaches and bays are low-rise resorts and beach hotels. Some recommended hotels are the Turtle Beach Hotel; Mount Irvine Bay Hotel, with its one-room Museum of Tobago History; and the Grafton Beach Resort in Black Rock. There are gift shops in the hotels and lots of sea-front vendors selling everything from shells to T-shirts to curried crab and dumplings.

Plymouth is the largest village on the northwest side of the island, just a short drive from Black Rock.

Interesting attractions at Plymouth include Fort James, the remnants of a rather small fort with a terrific view of Great Courland Bay, and the Arnos Vale Hotel, with winding trails through tropical trees. The Mot-Mot Trail is a good spot to view the mot-mot, a jaylike green bird with a blue head that is nicknamed the king of the forest. Another attraction is the mystery tombstone, a 1783 tombstone of one Betty Stiven which has a riddle inscribed upon it that supposedly has never been solved. The inscription reads: "Was a mother without knowing it, and a wife without letting her husband know it, except by her kind indulgence to him."

Now this riddle baffled us for a while, but eventually we figured it out. Betty Stiven meets a fellow and falls in love with him. But he refuses to marry her, and she won't live in sin. She then gets him so drunk that he passes out, and a preacher with a good sense of humor marries them. Betty, being a wife without her husband's knowledge, kindly indulges his every whim, and the result of one of those whims is that Betty becomes pregnant. But before she realizes she is pregnant, she is struck down by brain fever and goes into a coma. Without regaining consciousness, poor Betty comes to term and delivers a baby boy, but she dies during birth, "a mother without knowing it." So much for that riddle. We hope this revelation doesn't ruin Tobago's tourist industry.

From Plymouth, it's an easy drive over the hills to Scarborough, Tobago's capital and the largest town on the island (population 17,000). The downtown market square is a good place to begin exploring Scarborough. An indoor-outdoor market offers everything from salt cod to Shadow Bennie to clothing, and Lower Scarborough Mall has a wide assortment of shops.

One sight not to miss in Scarborough is Fort King George, an eighteenth-century fort, complete with cannons, which overlooks the capital and the southern coastline. The fort is well maintained, is beautifully landscaped, and houses a small art gallery and another Museum of Tobago History. The museum has Amerindian artifacts, fossils, and military implements from the various armies that occupied the fort during the years that Tobago changed hands so many times.

Scarborough has a small but interesting Botanic Station, which is nicely landscaped. Just off the approach highway from the airport, the station raises seedlings, such as Congo peppers, to supply small farmers. Southeast of Scarborough is Bacolet Beach, a palm-fringed, dark sand beach that was the setting for the movie *The Swiss Family Robinson*.

The food—particularly the seafood—is excellent in Scarborough and the western part of the island. Recommended restaurants are Dillon's at Crown Point, the Blue Crab on Robinson Street (try the kingfish or flying fish), the Old Donkey Cart House on Bacolet Street, and Neptune's at the Grafton Beach resort.

The Windward Road along the southern coast of Tobago leads the adventurous traveler to many natural wonders, the most obvious of which are the many beaches—almost all deserted. Two of the better beaches are at Hillsborough Bay and Barbadoes Bay. Farther along the coast, just after Belle Garden, is the Richmond Great House, a colonial plantation house that has been restored and is now a guesthouse and restaurant favored by nature lovers because of its beautiful setting.

Still farther along the Windward Road, at Roxborough, is the Argyll Waterfall, a three-part falls that is fun to climb. Roxborough is also the entryway to the the Tobago Forest Reserve—the oldest forest reserve in the Western Hemisphere, established by the British in 1764. Trips can be arranged by tour operators, but there's a fairly good road through it, the Parlatuvier-Roxborough Road. On the other side of Roxborough is King's Bay, with another waterfall and a small beach. Farther on is Speyside, where the Blue Waters Inn provides gear and guides for scuba diving. Just offshore is Tobago's largest bird sanctuary, Little Tobago.

Little Tobago Island is also called Bird of Paradise Island because forty-eight rare birds of paradise were brought there from New Guinea in 1909 by Sir William Ingram, who originally owned the island. Visitors can hire boats at Speyside for a short trip to Little Tobago (with prior permission from the game warden), but spotting a bird of paradise is not guaranteed. In 1963, Hurricane Flora inflicted severe damage to the bird habitats of Tobago, which have yet to recover fully, and the bird of paradise population has steadily declined. However, there are about sixty other species of birds on Little Tobago. Another bird sanctuary is the Melville Islands, off the eastern tip of Tobago. The largest of the

Melvilles, seventy-two-acre St. Giles, is an important seabird nesting ground for terns, boobies, and frigate birds.

The Windward Road continues from Speyside across Tobago's highest point, Flagstaff Hill, to Charlotteville, a picturesque fishing village. It is a four-mile trip that takes a half hour because of the switchbacks. Charlotteville has limited tourist facilities, but it's full of nature. Because of the greenery and the fact that bromeliads and orchids grow all over trees and wires, one guidebook suggested that "the effect is of being in an enormous misty terrarium."

Tobago's north coast is the most difficult place on the island to reach. Travelers must go all the way back to Roxborough for a trip across the Forest Reserve, since the road between Charlotteville and Parlatuvier is impassible. The other northern villages, such as Castara, are accessible only from Plymouth or Scarborough.

Hopefully this brief summary will give readers and vacationers an introduction to some of the better-known sights in T&T. For the sounds, once you set foot in T&T, all you have to do is listen—and then jump up!

jump up:
calypso and carnival

Music is so intimately linked with the history and culture of Trinidad and Tobago that to write about the country without mentioning calypso, steel band, and Carnival would be to ignore the soul of the country. And since music is inseparable from the spectacle of Carnival, the history of calypso, in many ways, is also the story of Carnival.

Despite its popularity today, the music of T&T did not gain instant acceptance. As steel band expert Pete Simon observed: "Both steel band and calypso had to run the gauntlet—from proscription to intolerance, to social disinheritance, to contempt, to snobbery and toleration, to patronage, to simulated acceptance, to full acceptance, and finally to total respect."

The Early Days

Even the very word "calypso" stimulates controversy. A spirited debate among musicologists has produced no fewer than ten separate theories about the origin of the word. First there is the obvious Greek connection—Calypso was the nymph who detained Odysseus in Homer's *The Odyssey*. Since Calypso was "the one who conceals," some experts say that the music was so-named because of its double-entendre lyrics. Others say that the word developed from the goddess Cariso, who was released from imprisonment because she could sing extemporaneously. Other theories attribute calypso to the French *carrousseaux*, a drinking party, or to the Spanish *caliso*, a topical song. Some experts have gone way out on a limb and claim that the word originated from the Calypso brand of insecticide that was sold in Trinidad!

But the most logical theory about the origin of the word holds that it has an African heritage. The musical style originated on the west coast of Africa as *kaiso*, which is a Hausa word meaning "bravo." The *kaiso* had a choral refrain, a dancing chorus, and a call-and-response structure. The style was closely linked to the Nigerian traditions of festivals where the whole community turned out and judged song contests performed by masqueraders. As Ernest Brown, a professor at Northeastern University who specializes in music, has observed: "Songs of ridicule are a powerful mechanism of social control, where royalty never appears without its praise singers." These African musical and festival traditions were the early heritage of calypso and Carnival, and they were transferred to T&T by slaves.

The African slaves, organized into work gangs, were encouraged by the plantation owners to compete against each other in the cutting of sugar cane. They sang *kaiso*-style work songs to increase productivity; the lead singer of the winning work gang bragged in song about his group's prowess and scorned the other gangs. The leaders adopted names such as Elephant and Thunderer, which were precursors to the colorful monikers of the later calypsonians. Eventually, the word *kaiso* became transformed into calypso.

In addition to work songs, the slaves sang songs of praise and derision. It is not surprising that the derisiveness was directed against the plantation owners. "There is no doubt that [the early] calypso songs were used like our spirituals here, as a clandestine means of spreading illegal knowledge among the slaves," wrote Paul Bowles in *Modern Music* in 1940.

"The slaves sang them in their tribal tongue, mocking their owners," observed Geoffrey Holder, a dancer and choreographer. "These frightfully, rightfully suspicious owners made the slaves learn Spanish, learn French, and finally learn English, to detect what was being said about them. The melodies became infected with Spanish, the dialect Creole, lastly English. What a melange!"

Oral history records that the first recognized Trinidadian calypsonian was Gros Jean, a professional singer who arrived in 1784 from Martinique with other French immigrants. He performed for slaveholder Pierre Bergorrat in a cave, praising his master and insulting his master's enemies. He was crowned, informally, "Gros Jean, Master of Kaiso," and thus became the first Calypso King.

Early calypso was strongly influenced by Spanish melodies from Venezuela, especially *parang*, a form of Christmas carol performed with guitar, *cuatro*, and mandolin. Around 1845, East Indian immigration added the *tassa* drumming style to the evolving musical tradition of T&T.

The arrival of the French not only signaled the formal beginning of calypso, but also of Carnival. The French celebrated with dinners, balls, fetes, and masquerades from Christmas to Ash Wednesday.

The emancipation of the slaves in the 1830s produced dramatic changes in both calypso and Carnival. Geoffrey Holder points out that the slaves had a tradition of contention in song, and after they were freed, since they had no owners to mock, they started mocking themselves. "They blackmailed themselves in song," he wrote.

The former slaves also began celebrating Carnival, but with a twist. They turned elegant bourgeois balls into street parties, as they partied heartily at *canboulay*, the burning off of the cane fields on the plantations. In 1838, the newspapers reported that the freed slaves had taken to the streets and were singing calypsos in *patois* while carrying a stuffed dummy of a woman on a pole—perhaps the first masquerade road march ever in Trinidad.

The *canboulay* celebrations often got out of hand when the freed slaves practiced stick fighting, which was considered an art form by them, but was deemed threatening by the planting class. Rival *kalenda* bands, as they were called, each led by a *chantwell*, or lead singer, roamed the streets of Port of Spain during Carnival. When two bands met, the *chantwells* would trade insults in song before the stick fighting began:

> Rain can't wet me,
> When I have my *poui* (fighting stick) in my hand.
> Rain can't wet me,
> I am advancing on the foe like a roaring lion!

Since the *kalenda* bands were judged not for their musical ability but for their offensive strength, bloody battles were waged among the bands. The government attempted to regulate the celebrators, and in 1868 a law was passed prohibiting the singing of profane songs or ballads. But by 1870 the *canboulay* celebrations had completely dominated the genteel fetes and were so rowdy that they were described in the newspapers of the day as "an unremitting uproar, yelling, drumming, and blowing of horns." The participants were "hordes of disreputable males and females . . . organized into bands and societies for the maintenance of vagrancy, immorality, and vice."

The press predicted the end of Carnival, which nearly came to pass in 1881, when the police decided to crack down on the celebrators. A posse of police clashed with the stick-fighting bands of calypsonians, and the infamous Canboulay Riot ensued. Carnival was ruined that year, and the resulting investigation began the government's attack on calypso. The beating of skin drums became forbidden, because the upper class believed that the sound of the drums "drove the blacks into a frenzy."

In 1884 the British government of Trinidad banned all drumming after calypso, and Carnival came under attack, not only from the police and courts but also from the press and the church. Both the Africans and the East Indians rioted to protest the drumming ban, which revealed the increasing links between the cultures as a result of a common love of music. Later, various Carnival masquerade figures were banned because the authorities believed that they also incited the crowds to riot.

The ban on drumming caused the innovative musicians to improvise, and the result was *tamboo-bamboo* bands (*tamboo* was derived from the French *tambour*, a drum). Large-bore sections of cured bamboo were whacked with smaller sticks to make a rich, polyrhythmic effect. The bamboo sections were also stamped on the ground to produce a bass sound. Since the *tamboo*-bamboo bands were not technically using drums, they were allowed to perform, and Carnival went on!

The government, however, was still antidrum and eventually banned even the *tamboo*-bamboo bands. Percussion disappeared completely from calypso for more than a half-century. As a further indication of the government's suspicions, in 1893 a British warship sailed into the Port of Spain harbor as a precautionary measure against violence at Carnival. Ironically, the ship was the sixteen-gun H.M.S. *Calypso*.

The Evolution of an Art Form

By the turn of the twentieth century, calypsos were being sung in English rather than *patois*, and the first completely English calypso was performed by Norman Le Blanc, a white calypsonian. Music historian Ernest Brown pointed out: "After 100 years of British rule, the English language was finally understood widely enough to be used in a popular song." The turn of the century also marked the first use of the word *calipso* in the *Port of Spain Gazette*.

For the first time, the middle and upper classes began to take an interest in calypso, and businesses started sponsoring competitions. White and mixed-race calypsonians appeared with greater frequency;

they were called jacketmen because they wore jackets to indicate their higher social status. Although Venezuelan string bands influenced the musical styles of the day, *tamboo*-bamboo percussion was still the predominant sound.

Calypso songs changed from a call-and-response form to an oratorical style that featured seven- and eight-line stanzas, which were more direct because they presented the ideas in a step-by-step manner. This style was preferred by early calypsonians such as Atilla the Hun (Raymond Quevedo), Lord Executor (Philip Garcia), and Chieftan Douglas. These singers also began to infuse their songs with politics rather than just gossip and scandal.

The calypsonians relished competition with their peers and took pride in their own poetic abilities while disparaging those of others. As Lord Executor sang to Atilla the Hun:

> I admire your ambition, you'd like to sing,
> But you will never be a *kaiso* king.
> To reach such a height without a blemish or spot
> You must study Shakespeare, Byron, Milton, and
>   Scott.
> But I'm afraid I'm casting pearls before swine,
> For you'll never inculcate such thoughts divine.
> You really got a good intention, but poor education.

In 1906 Lionel Belasco, one of the Caribbean's foremost composers, performed his "Le Anne Passe," a catchy tune about a little girl who grew up to be a streetwalker. Not only did this song contain calypso's first historical reference to a prostitute, it also would be featured in a lawsuit decades later.

Belasco was the star of the first calypso recordings by the Victor Gramaphone Company in 1914. A crew of technicians traveled to Trinidad and recorded Belasco's band; eventually Belasco recorded more than three hundred songs for Decca, Columbia, and other companies.

By 1920, anti-British sentiments were appearing in calypso, and police spies would sit in on calypso performances to spot the offenders who were belittling the Crown. A calypsonian named Patrick Jones was nearly indicted for sedition by singing:

> Britain boasts of democracy,
> Brotherly love and fraternity,
> But British colonists have ruled in perpetual
>   misery.

The following year marked the appearance of the first calypso tent. Erected by Chieftain Douglas for the entertainment of his own fans, this tent was independent of the marching masquerade bands. The practice caught on, and in 1929 syndicates or cooperatives of calypsonians began charging admission to tents and soliciting businesses to sponsor them. The names of the bands of the day were very colorful: the Roman Emperors, the Phillistine Warriors, The Mummies of Tutankhamen's Tomb, and The Abyssinians.

Around this time, radio was becoming popular in both the United States and Trinidad, and that medium provided another venue for calypsonians. In the United States, Americans heard their first calypso on the radio: "Sly Mongoose," a Sam Manning song recorded by Paul Whiteman.

Some calypsonians disliked recorded calypso because it was not spontaneous. As The Gorilla explained:

> Calypso is a thing I'm telling you
> When you are singing, you must learn to impromptu.
> Never mind your English, but mind your rhymes,
> When you get the gist of it, just sing in time,
> For veteran calypsonians are known to be
> Men who can sing on anything instantaneously.

Since all known calypso songs are based on fewer than fifty melodies, tradition held that the lyrics must be fresh and clever. Obviously, calypso records could not achieve that kind of spontaneity, but they could and did spread the message of the composer.

Through radio and performance, calypso evolved into, as the Mighty Panther (Vernon Roberts) described it, "the voice of the people in Trinidad, the newspaper of the common man." Roberts went on to observe that, "A calypsonian in Trinidad has no respect for rank or station; he'll sing against the governor or anybody if he has something to say." Geoffrey Holder notes: "True calypso tells a story very close to the everyday lives of the people. . . . It is the music of strugglers struggling."

And struggle they did. Despite the popularity of calypso among the common folk, the British government had never ceased its harassment of the art. During the 1930s, police began enforcing the old 1868 law against the singing of "profane" songs. Atilla the Hun (Quevedo) responded elegantly:

To say these songs are sacrilegious, obscene or
  profane
Is only a lie and a dirty shame.
If the calypso is indecent then I must insist,
So is Shakespeare's "Venus and Adonis,"
Boccaccio's tales, Voltaire's *Candide,*
The Martyrdom of Man by Winwood Reid,
Yet over these authors they make no fuss,
But they want to take advantage of us.

Quevedo had the last laugh: he was elected to
the Trinidad Legislative Council in 1950 and later
became deputy mayor of Port of Spain.

In 1934 Trinidadian calypso entered the modern
era when Atilla the Hun and The Lion (Hubert
Charles) signed with Decca Records. Thousands of
fans crowded the Port of Spain docks to see them off
to New York. Rudy Valle and Bing Crosby attended
their recording sessions, and The Lion's calypso
"Ugly Woman" was broadcast live on Valle's NBC
radio show. The Lion's succinct and tongue-in-
cheek advice was the following:

If you want to be happy and live a king's life,
Never make a pretty woman your wife . . .
From a logical point of view,
Always marry a woman uglier than you.

(This calypso was later renamed "If You Want To
Be Happy," and became a hit in the United States for
Jimmy Soul in 1963.) Upon their return from New
York, Atilla the Hun sang about their recent fame:

When you sing *kaiso* in Trinidad,
You are a vagabond and everything that's bad.
In your native land you are a hooligan—
In New York, you are an artiste and a gentleman.
For instance, take The Lion and me
Having dinner with Rudy Vallee.

Despite the prestige of Atilla and Lion, the British colonial government passed the Dance Halls
Ordinance in 1934, giving the police power to cen-
sor the text of songs and giving the colonial secre-
tary the right to ban any record. The licensing of
calypsonians for singing was soon enacted, and the
public dissension, as a result of the ordinance, was
a harbinger of the first stirrings of independence
from England. But with their usual aplomb,
calypsonians shrugged off the ordinances. In 1938
The Caresser (Rufus Calender) sang:

The more they try to do me bad
The better I live in Trinidad.

To fight oppression, the calypsonians did what
all downtrodden people do—they organized. The
first group of professional calypsonians became
known as the Old Brigade; it included the singers
Lion and Atilla, plus Growling Tiger, Lord Pretender,
King Radio, and Lord Beginner.

Around the time that the Old Brigade was organ-
izing, a new musical movement was beginning in
Trinidad, one that would sweep away any remaining
prejudice against music on the island.

It all began with Alexander's Ragtime Band, led
by Lord Humbugger, dressed only in a top hat and
a long black overcoat. On Carnival Monday morning
in 1937, this band paraded through the streets of
Port of Spain beating on metal "instruments"—
brake drums, garbage can covers, wheel rims, and
buckets—with steel rods.

The metallic ring of steel electrified the crowds,
who jumped up and joined the band as it swept down
Frederick Street. "The compelling rhythm had
touched a hidden chord dormant all those years,"
wrote music historian Pete Simon. "The revellers
recognized it as a call reaching out to them across
centuries of time." Percussion had returned to calypso.

The use of metal percussion increased at Carnival each year until the beginning of World War II,
when the event was canceled for security reasons.
The years 1941 through 1945 became known as the
time of "no mas," which is a typical Caribbean pun
meaning, in English, "no masquerade," and in Spanish, "no more."

The cancellation of Carnival angered the people,
but it did not stop the interest in metal percussion.
In fact, the art was revolutionized: the U.S. forces
stationed at the bases of Chaguaramas and Waller
Field had brought with them the next incarnation of
metal percussion—steel oil drums.

Inventive musicians such as Neville Jules cut the
drums in various lengths. The bottom surfaces of
these lengths were heated and hammered into separate bumps, each producing a different note when
struck. The longer the cut drums, the lower the
notes. By experimenting, the musicians made steel
drums that created a wide range of sounds.

The steel drum is the only musical instrument
invented during the twentieth century. Its influence
on the music and culture of T&T has been profound.
Music historian Daniel Crowley has noted: "Here is

a complex art form created by lower-class, ill-educated, underprivileged adolescents against the will of their parents, the ruling class, and the police."

In addition to providentially providing steel drums, the U.S. presence in T&T during the war years greatly influenced the history of calypso. The music had its second flurry of interest in the United States in 1939 when Wilmoth Houdini, a Brooklyn-born calypsonian, recorded "Stone Cold Dead in the Market Place," which was the first big calypso hit in the states. So the servicemen stationed in Trinidad were somewhat familiar with the style of music, and although Carnival was canceled, they could still listen to singers such as The Growler (Errol Duke) sing about the meat shortage in 1943:

I think I got to make a firm determination
To stop eating beef in this meat depression.
For we can't get cattle and we can't get hog
And my mind only telling me I'm eating dog;
Beef and pork was always me line,
So them wolfhound wouldn't eat out me intestine.

The influx of U.S. military personnel meant higher wages for Trinis, but it also meant an increase in promiscuity and prostitution. Ironically, the latter produced a hit song that was pirated from Port of Spain and prostituted in the United States! In 1944, American comic Morey Amsterdam heard a catchy calypso tune while in Trinidad. It was Lord Invader's (Rupert Grant's) version of "Rum and Coca Cola," a satirical song about prostitution between U.S. soldiers and Trini women:

Since the Yankees come to Trinidad,
They have the young girls going mad.
The girls say they treat them nice,
And they give them a better price.
They buy rum and Coca Cola.
Go down to Point Cumana.
Both mother and daughter
Working for the Yankee dollar.

Believing the song to be in the public domain, Amsterdam arranged to have it adapted for the American market by Jeri Sullavan and Paul Baron; he added some lyrics himself. The song made its debut at the Versailles night club in New York as sung by Jeri Sullavan, and in the following year, 1945, "Rum and Coca Cola" was an enormous hit for the Andrews Sisters on the Decca label, selling more than 200,000 copies.

However, the American "composers" of the song were sued for plagiarism by Lionel Belasco, author of a music folio entitled *Calypso Songs of the West Indies*, and the composer of "L'Anne Passe." Remember him from 1906? Belasco and the folio's publisher, Maurice Baron, a noted composer and conductor, charged that "L'Anne Passe" was the original melody for the song "Rum and Coca Cola."

The attorney for the plaintiff, Louis Nizer, won a substantial monetary settlement for Belasco. Rumors spread that Lord Invader had shared in the settlement (some said $100,000, a large sum in those days). Later, so the story went, Grant opened a night club in Port of Spain and gave away drinks (presumably rum and Coca Cola) until his money ran out.

After World War II, music in T&T began to evolve quickly. The 1946 Carnival, the first after the years of "no mas," featured concerts of solely steel drums for the first time. These drums now had fourteen notes apiece, and the music made with them was increasingly sophisticated. Attitudes about music had changed considerably, and now calypso and steel band were getting respect as the Trinis inched toward independence from England and took pride in their own culture.

Soon after the war ended, a number of younger calypsonians, known as the Young Brigade, started singing more about sex and fantasy than about political events. Lord Kitchener (Aldwin Roberts), Mighty Killer, and Lord Wonder were all members of the New Brigade; they said they were going to "mash up the Old Brigade." The Old Brigade responded by monopolizing the tents and not letting the Young Brigade perform. But the Young Brigade simply opened their own tents and became popular as well.

By the late 1940s, calypso had spread far and wide throughout the Caribbean, which led to stories that calypso had not originated in Trinidad, but in tourist destinations such as Jamaica, the Virgin Islands, or the Bahamas. The Jamaica Tourist Board even used the slogan "Land of Calypso" in its advertising. Despite such hype, there is no doubt that calypso's only home is Trinidad. As musicologist Daniel Crowley insists, "For a Jamaican or a Virgin Islander to claim modern calypso as its own is tantamount to a Swede or Scot claiming Italian opera."

Inspired by calypso songs on the radio, Americans began to visit T&T in greater numbers. Even scientists ventured onto the islands, much to the delight of the calypsonians, who mocked them. The Mighty Panther sang of a bald anthropologist:

> See the professor sitting there,
> He looking like a millionaire.
> He making all the people feel small,
> 'Cause he got a head like a cannonball!

The Heyday of Calypso

The 1950s were a volatile decade for calypso. It all began in 1950 with a British travel writer, Patrick Fermor, calling calypso "the only living folk music—at any rate in English—in the British Empire." That same year marked the first steel-band competition at Carnival; the next year, the Trinidad and Tobago All-Steel Percussion Orchestra toured Britain, to great popular acclaim.

Following the popular trend of calypso, in 1953 in the United States a little known, Jamaican-born folk singer recorded his first calypso for RCA Victor. The song was called "Matilda, Matilda," and the singer's name was Harry Belafonte. Two years later, in October 1955, Belafonte was crooning the catchy song on NBC-TV's special "Holiday in Trinidad."

The biggest year for calypso was 1956. A *Time* magazine article on Carnival in Port of Spain observed: "During Carnival there is scarcely a person—save a few fusty English colonials in temporary retirement on quieter islands nearby—who does not 'jump up' to the stimulating rhythms."

Also that same year, Mighty Sparrow (Slinger Francisco) won the first of many crowns as calypso king. His winning song was "Yankees Gone" (now called "Jean and Dinah"), about the closing of the U.S. naval base at Chaguaramas. It featured risqué lyrics and a familiar topic:

> Well the girls in town feeling bad
> No more Yankees in Trinidad.
> They going to close down the base for good
> Them girls got to make out how they could.
> Is now they park up in town
> In for a penny, in for a pound.
> Yes is competition for so
> Trouble in town when the price drop so low.

The year 1956 also witnessed the release of Harry Belafonte's LP *Calypso* on the RCA Victor label. Hit singles from the album included "Banana Boat Song" and "Jamaica Farewell." *Calypso* was the first long-playing record by a solo artist to sell a million copies in the United States; it was the number one LP for thirty-one weeks.

Interestingly enough, most of the songs were not true calypsos but Jamaican-style ballads. As one critic put it, "A man singing calypso with a Jamaican accent, as does Harry Belafonte, is no true calypso man. For one thing, and the chief thing, he is not singing a song that he himself created impromptu. He is, instead, a balladeer or folk singer; in this case, a Jamaican folk singer."

Belafonte admitted that he was no calypsonian in *Newsweek* in 1957. "Two of my big records right now are not even calypso," he said. "'Jamaica Farewell' is a West Indian folk ballad and 'Day-O,' which is called 'Banana Boat Song,' is a West Indian work song." Despite his admission, he defended his art. "It is any artist's right to interpret the subject matter as he sees fit," he told music critic Jay Harrison of the *New York Herald Tribune*. Belafonte also showed his contempt for traditional calypso: "Listen, if I wanted to sing pure calypso, I could have. . . . But that kind of material does not reflect the dignity of the people, and the calypso I sing, even in my own version, does show the people."

It is interesting to note that American folk singers strongly influenced the perception of calypso around the world. They polished it for popular consumption. Performers such as Harry Belafonte implied with their style of singing that calypso music was strongly linked to the folk music rage in the United States. However, when we listen to calypsos recorded between 1912 and 1940 in Trinidad, it is clear that any American influence on the music came not from folk music, but from Dixieland, Swing, and Big Band music.

Other American so-called calypso challengers became popular. The Kingston Trio had a hit with "Zombie Jamboree," another calypso made famous by Lord Invader. It had the familiar phrase "back to back and belly to belly and we don't give a damn 'cause we done that already." Rosemary Clooney had a Tin Pan Alley calypso hit with "Mangos, Papaya" on Columbia. That label was also battling RCA's Belafonte dominance with The Easy Riders, who had a smash hit with "Marianne," the same tune made popular by The Lion more than a decade earlier; however, most Americans had no idea what the lyrics meant:

> All day, all night, Marianne
> Down by the seaside, sifting sand.

Marianne, of course, was a prostitute, and the sand was a metaphor for her numerous customers!

Trinidadians were understandably concerned about the American commercialization of their art and the fact that non-Trinidadians had hijacked their calypso music. Mighty Panther (Vernon Roberts), who was the Calypso King in 1953-54, told big band leader Les Brown in *Down Beat* magazine: "A Calypsonian is a natural composer of lyric and melody but not a musician. He is a primitive who knows nothing about music. But he's able to compose a story on any subject, whether it be commonplace or fantasy. A commercial Calypso singer is a parasite—he only sings what he memorizes."

Roberts pointed out that many of the calypso "standards" of the fifties had deeper roots. The familar "Matilda," sung by Harry Belafonte (virtually his theme song), had been introduced by King Radio (Norman Span) in 1925, and had probably been kept alive by the oral tradition and perhaps some recorded versions. The refrain is one of the most memorable of Trindadian songs in the United States: "Matilda, she take me money and she run Venezuela."

In 1957 calypso music took the United States by storm. Belafonte and his imitators were riding high, and the music was a full-fledged fad. In an article entitled "Calypsomania," *Time* magazine reported that music stores were selling do-it-yourself calypso kits, complete with bongo drums, a gourd, and a pair of maracas. Hollywood was considering a dozen calypso films, including one with the improbable title of *Calypso Grips So.* Calypso night clubs opened on the U.S. East Coast, including The Jamaican Room on New York's Third Avenue.

Not everyone was happy with this pseudo-calypso. Ann Elliott, a native Trinidadian who covered the 1957 Carnival for *Dance* magazine, wrote that in the eyes of Trinidadians, "Americans were dancing calypso as though it were a bastard hula-cum-samba and that they were mouthing calypso in the most disgusting and illiterate manner." Columnist Dorothy Kilgallen reported that two calypso song writers, Diane Lampert and John Gluck, Jr., had written more than twenty-five calypsos but had "never set foot in Trinidad or any other island."

Another momentous 1957 event was that "Banana Boat Song" hit the British pop charts and eventually rose to number three, while sparking a British calypso craze. Many music trade magazines in the States hinted that perhaps rock and roll was dead and would be replaced by West Indian calypso. Harry Belafonte called rock and roll "musical trash," although he did modestly admit that he "didn't want to be known as the guy who put the nail in the coffin of rock and roll."

Well, the death of rock and roll was announced a bit prematurely; ironically, the victim was calypso instead—at least in the United States. Just as suddenly as it began, the craze was over. By the end of 1957, calypso was, to quote the first calypso hit in the United States, "stone cold dead in the marketplace."

Calypso Transformed

The major effect of the American calypso craze on Trinidadian calypso was to bring it into the commercial world. Trini calypsonians now realized the power of mass media and state-of-the-art recording techniques and began to use them. Increasingly, calypso was becoming more of a recording art than a performing art.

During this time, American music became popular on T&T radio stations and was threatening to eclipse the traditional calypsos. In order to compete, Mighty Sparrow, who became calypso's primary spokesman during the 1960s, changed with the times and elevated dance-style music to a status equal with the humorous lyric. And his lyrics dealt less with politics and more with Carnival ("Don't Back Back"), sex ("Ah Afraid Pussy" and "Sixty-Nine"), and social situations. In "Drunk and Disorderly," for example, he sang:

> They never teach me rum control
> So put as long as meh glass could hold.
> They say a hungry man is an angry man
> But a drinking man is a happy man.

"Sparrow transformed calypso by infusing it with ideas lifted deftly and selectively from the competition, American pop," wrote music critic Daisann

McLane. And once again, calypso traditionalists were not pleased. The Mighty Chalkdust, a history scholar, complained:

If you want to win the crown,
Sing about wine, women, and song.
Sing about your neighbor's wife,
Sing about your own sex life.

But many music critics believe that the "commercialization" of calypso was inevitable. "At various times calypso backings have favored Venezuelan music, jazz, Cuban touches, and rhythm and blues," observes music historian John Storm Roberts. "But like any strongly based and original music, it has benefitted from these rather than being swamped. Similarly, it has been under fairly steady attack ever since at least the late 1930s for having gone commercial. It seems that the latest but one generation of calypsonians is always the last true one." Incidentally, Chalkdust continued singing about politics and eventually became a rival for best calypsonian, competing well against Sparrow and Lord Kitchener and winning the Calypso King award in 1981.

Interestingly enough, the emphasis on dancing and partying in calypso music actually accelerated the popularity of Carnival and the competition for Calypso King (also called Calypso Monarch). In 1969, for example, 250 calypsonians were auditioned, and each singer had two original compositions—an enormous output of creativity. During this time, the interest in steel band music actually declined as the steel bands lost touch with the masquerade bands and began to play more classical music.

Mighty Sparrow regained his title of Calypso King in 1972 and won again in '73 and '74, becoming the first three-time consecutive winner in history. He continued to adapt to the times and became the primary influence on the transition of calypso into what is now called *soca*.

This time, there was no confusion about the name of a T&T music form. *Soca* was a fusion of soul and calypso, both in name and sound. It was designed to be recorded as much as performed, and it successfully competed with American soul and disco music, which were popular on the West Indian radio stations.

In early 1993 there were numerous superstars of *soca*. The Mighty Sparrow is still going strong, but David Rudder has been hot on his trail, winning the Calypso King title in 1986 with his song "Bahia Girl." His string of hits includes Road Song favorites "The Hammer" and "This Party Is It!" Two other popular *soca* superstars are Arrow (Alphonsus Cassell), famous for his energetic party songs, and Tambu (Chris Herbert), the driving force behind the excellent *Culture* album.

Despite being international stars, these *soca* artists are criticized for being overly commercial. "They are taking the money in one hand," accused the Mighty Chalkdust, "and losing their culture through the fingers of the other."

Then again, *soca* has been defended against such charges by music critic Daisann McLane: "*Soca* is not really all that different from traditional calypso, it is simply calypso modified to a particular market."

Chalkdust's worries notwithstanding, it is unlikely that T&T will ever lose its musical culture or forget its musical heritage. Trinidadians remember the words of Albert Gomes, a politician who struggled against British imperialism, who wrote in 1950: "Long after most of us are forgotten, certain calypsos will survive as the only reminders to some later generation of how we lived, loved, laboured, and sinned."

The art of pure, improvised calypso is not lost in T&T—we know that from personal experience. At an overlook on our way to Maracas Bay, we were serenaded by a calypsonian with only a ukelele, who improvised a calypso that neatly skewered us in satirical rhymes. Mary Jane was described as a teacher (she was one for seventeen years) and Dave as an advertising man (he was one for fifteen years).

Soca may have far eclipsed this improvised, traditional calypso style, but it has also enabled calypso artists to break out of T&T and into the world to a much greater extent than the calypso artists of the forties and fifties. However, although *soca* was thought to be the next big Caribbean music rage, it has never achieved the popularity of reggae around the world. Reggae, the Jamaican music of revolution, appeals to rock audiences that identify with its politically correct stance. *Soca*, on the other hand, is now considered to be pure party music. "It simply works as a valve, a tension release," explains Daisann McLane. "Pop music as group therapy."

And since part of the therapy of Carnival is to party, *soca* fits in perfectly. In the words of the Mighty Douglas:

> You got the great big long wall in China,
> And the Indian Taj Mahal,
> I know that the greatest wonder of them all
> Is my Trinidad Carnival.

The Ultimate Party

"If we could channel half the thought, devotion, and energy that we produce for Carnival into economic production," wrote Andrew Carr in 1975, "Trinidad and Tobago would become one of the most productive countries in the world."

Carr's observation is only slightly exaggerated, since Carnival is such a mammoth spectacle that it requires many months to plan and many thousands of people to produce. Many observers believe that T&T's Carnival is the finest such celebration in the world, eclipsing even the Mardi Gras parades and parties in New Orleans and Rio de Janiero.

One reason for the spectacular success of T&T's Carnival is that it springs directly from the people and is not organized by the government or private industry. Rather, ten to fifteen clubs devote themselves to the designing and building of the elaborate costumes. Each club has hundreds of loyal members, and the ranks swell up to as many as 3,000 people during Carnival when friends join in to play *mas*, and the club becomes a band.

Two definitions are in order. Playing "mas" (short for masquerade) refers to the entire spectacle of dressing up in costume, singing, and dancing. A carnival "band" is not just the musicians, but rather all the people who have gathered together to produce the spectacle: the dancers, musicians, and the frenetic public that joins in.

The Carnival process begins, surprisingly enough, with research. After the subject or theme is decided, the clubs must research their costume designs to ensure that they are authentic. Recent themes have included "Merrie England," "Wonders of Buccoo Reef," and "Bright Africa."

After the research and design are completed, the clubs spend months assembling the raw materials—everything from velvet to feathers—and often constructing, at their "*mas* camps," huge, elaborate costumes resembling floats for their kings and queens. No matter how large or cumbersome, a costume cannot be motorized, pushed, or pulled, so it must be designed so that it can be carried by one person. The clubs must also fashion hundreds of matching, supporting costumes for band members.

The result of all this effort, energy, and expense is a few days of intense bacchanalia. In the words of Molly Ahye: "A kaleidoscopic display of musical and artistic creativity, of high-spirited camaraderie and hedonistic beauty, it opens the floodgates to unbridled self-expression, a spectacle of color, movement, music, sensuality and the lavish joy of life which seems a hallmark of Trinidad and Tobago."

Although clubs begin work on the next year's Carnival on Ash Wednesday, the day after Carnival, most of the pre-Carnival activities in T&T don't begin until right after New Year's Day. Then the calypso tents open up, which are actually enclosed stages located in stadiums and cricket fields. The calypso and *soca* musicians begin practicing, and schedules for the tents and their performers are printed in the newspapers.

Although there are some preliminary "pan" (steel drum), calypso, and "mas" competitions, the push toward Carnival really gets going after February 1. Events and locations change from year to year, but we've attempted to piece together a rough schedule, as follows.

Depending on the dates of Carnival, which are dependent on the date of Easter, in late January or February the first panorama preliminaries and the Traditional Carnival Character Festival are held in several different cities.

The National and Zonal Preliminaries of both "pan" and calypso follow, in various locations around T&T, with another Carnival Character Festival in San Fernando. Next comes the National Calypso Semifinals in San Fernando and the National Panorama Semifinals at the Queen's Park Savannah in Port of Spain. Just prior to Carnival, the National Panorama Finals are held at Queen's Park Savannah; the Traditional Carnival Character Festival also makes its appearance there.

The first Carnival day (actually night) is Dimanche Gras, "fat Sunday," the Sunday night before Ash Wednesday. This is the night for private parties all over T&T—at homes, restaurants, night clubs, and hotels. Some of the fetes attract thousands of people. At the Queen's Park Savannah is a big show featuring the Calypso King finals, the finals for king and queen of Carnival, and the award for best panorama steel band. (Some of these events occasionally occur earlier than Sunday night.) The Dimanche Gras festivities usually extend all night long for the truly devoted revellers, who remember the words of Growling Tiger (Neville Marcano) in 1941:

> Fete and bacchanal,
> Who the devil can stop Creole carnival?

Dimanche Gras actually blends into Jour Overt, or *joovay* (Carnival Monday), which begins at 4 a.m. with road marches featuring steel bands and old African "mas" characters. Daisann McLane described the early morning road march: "There is something magical about parading through dawn-lit streets surrounded by dancing jumbies . . . you drift off gently into the Caribbean morning like a child waking from a marvelous dream."

Also on *joovay*, the massive parade of bands (also called a road march) is held at about one in the afternoon, and bands must march past judging stands usually at Independence Square, Victoria Square, Adam Smith Square, and end up at the Queen's Park Savannah. The costumes are not as elaborate as they will be for Mardi Gras, and they emphasize the humorous rather than the spectacular. As one witness describes it: "Mainly this is the time of the festival devoted to the comic and the satirical; the grotesque; the double entendre and the ribald, and occasionally the obscene."

On Mardi Gras, "Fat Tuesday," the entire parade process begins again at the same locations—but this time starting at nine o'clock in the morning. Now the costumes are elaborate: "Marvelous creatures—dragons, birds, gigantic flowers, castles, chariots, ships—go by in endless variety, the only visibly human thing about them are the little dancing feet just showing under the towering structure," in the words of Andrew Carr. Visitors can pay about fifty U.S. dollars to wear a costume and join a band, but it costs nothing for anyone watching to jump up. As poet and playwright Derek Walcott explained: "Carnival is all that is claimed for it. It is exultation of the mass will, its hedonism is so sacred that to withdraw from it, not to jump up, to be a contemplative outside of its frenzy is a heresy."

And what does all this spectacle mean? The question was put to Peter Minshall, the Trinidadian who designed part of the opening ceremonies for the 1992 Olympic Games in Barcelona and T&T's premier "mas" designer who once created a band called Papillon, composed of 3,000 human butterflies.

"Trinidad Carnival is a form of theatre," Minshall said, "except that the costume assumes dominance, so that what you wear is no longer a costume. It becomes a sculpture, whether it is a puppet or a great set of wings, and once you put a human being into it, it begins to dance. This is my discipline. I have the streets, the hot midday sun. I have 2,000 to 3,000 people moving to music. And I put colors, shapes, and form on these people, and they pass in front of the viewers like a visual symphony. The artist in Carnival becomes the medium through which people express themselves."

The revellers must drink and eat. Writer Ann Elliot recalled, as a child, sitting outside calypso tents just before Carnival: "We were given delicious morsels of things to eat: pastello (corn wrapped around meat and steamed in a plantain leaf), pelau (a cook-up of rice and meat), crab-back (crabs taken out of the shell, mixed with all kinds of fragrant herbs, sprinkled with bread crumbs and red salt butter, and baked au gratin)."

In the words of *soca* artist Tambu (Chris Herbert):

> Whenever you lose your energy
> We have a good remedy
> Blue food with some dumplings
> Crab and callaloo
> Or ah bake and salt fish
> That bound to help you
> To put back what you lost
> Try a beef roti or ah glass of seamoss
> Then is back to party!

"makaforshet":
food traditions

"To understand Trinidad, it is essential you know her foods and live by them," wrote the famous Trini cook Jean de Boissiere. His 1948 book, *Cooking Creole*, was a noble attempt to preserve the Creole method of cooking, which had developed for centuries in Trinidad and Tobago. De Boissiere probably described some of his cooking as *makaforshet*, an early calypso term for food. The word was derived from the French phrase *ma ca fourchette*, meaning "food stuck between the fork" or, by implication, food that lives on.

By tasting the food that lives on in T&T, we can experience culinary history firsthand, for the country has the most varied and interesting cuisine of any of the islands in the West Indies. No fewer than seven distinctly different cultures have influenced this medley of the culinary arts, and it is a tribute to the spirit of the people that this cuisine has remained mostly intact—despite the influence of American fast foods.

Native Origins

The people who originated Trinidadian cuisine were, of course, the Amerindians—specifically, the Arawaks who migrated from Venezuela thousands of years ago in large dugout canoes. They lived by hunting, fishing, farming, and gathering the fruits and vegetables that grew wild on the island. Archaeological evidence indicates that they consumed more than forty types of fish and shellfish, including the *cascadura*, a primitive, armor-plated, mud-dwelling river fish that is a survivor from the Silurian age. Legend holds that anyone who eats the *cascadura* will always return to Trinidad.

The other seafood they consumed included shark, grouper, lobsters, oysters, turtle, shrimp, conch, crab, and chip-chip, a small mollusk. One of the more ingenious ways the Arawaks fished was to capture a remora, the fish that attaches itself to sharks and other large fish by means of a sucker disk on the top of its head. The Amerindians, seated in a canoe, would tie a cord to a remora's tail and release the fish when a turtle came near the canoe. After the remora attached to the turtle, they would pull both up to the canoe, where the turtle was easily captured.

The Arawaks hunted birds, deer, armadillos, iguanas, tortoises, peccaries, and agoutis. The meat was usually boiled in clay pots or smoked on a platform of green tree branches called a *brabacot*— a word that the Spanish changed to *barbacao* and was eventually Anglicized to "barbecue." Some of the basic vegetables and fruits grown were cassava and yams, root crops now called "ground provisions" in T&T. Other favorite crops were melons, pumpkins, papayas, plantains, maize, and hot chile peppers, which were often combined into a spicy gruel. Corn was ground into meal, then made into a dough, which was then baked over coals in corn husks. This dish was the earliest form of corn bread.

Cassava was one of the staples of the Arawak diet, and it came in two varieties, sweet and bitter. The bitter variety contained large amounts of poisonous prussic acid, which had to be extracted (by cooking or pressing) before the roots could be consumed. The Arawaks discovered that if this poisonous juice was boiled, it was rendered into a harmless, thick substance called *cassareep*, which was an excellent preservative for meat. This discovery led to the invention of a stew called pepperpot, which is still an island favorite today. We have heard stories of some pepperpots that have continued for years, if not generations, by the periodic addition of more ingredients and *cassareep*.

The European Invasion

The simple Amerindian life-style was forever changed, beginning in 1498, when Columbus landed on Trinidad. Although we cannot blame the demise of the Amerindians on a single individual, in little more than a century after his "discovery" of Trinidad, the Arawaks were wiped out by disease (especially smallpox), slavery, and war with the Caribs—a warlike tribe that inhabited Tobago and other islands in the Caribbean. Nevertheless calypso celebrated Columbus in 1926 with a tune that is still remembered today:

> Were you not told what Columbus saw
> When he landed on here shore,
> He saw the Caribs so brave and bold,
> The hummingbirds with their wings of gold,
> He was so glad that he called the island Trinidad.

Today, a small settlement of mixed-blood Amerindians at Arima is all that is left of the thousands of Arawaks and Caribs who first inhabited Trinidad. Ironically, though, the most popular beer in T&T is the Carib brand.

In 1592, the Spanish adventurer Antonio de Berrio founded the first European settlement on Trinidad at San Jose de Oruña (today St. Joseph), but the island was not seriously settled by the Spanish until the late 1600s. The earliest settlers were planters who grew mostly cocoa and tobacco. They introduced peas, beans, oranges, limes, and dried meats and fish. A culinary legacy of the Spanish settlement is *pastelles*, a type of tamale wrapped in banana leaves that is traditionally served at Christmastime—as are tamales in Mexico and the southwestern United States. But Trinidad was a distant outpost of the Spanish empire, and in 1662 the Spanish governor wrote to the king that no Spanish ship had visited the island for more than thirty years!

On Tobago in the 1600s, the Dutch were entrenched on their sugar-cane plantations. But the British ousted the Dutch and periodically occupied the island, as did other countries. It is said that Tobago changed hands more often than any other island in the Caribbean—at least two dozen times! So great was the dispute over this tiny island that it was declared a no man's land in 1684 and subsequently became a haven for pirates and remained so until the British were finally granted control by the Treaty of Paris in 1763. The French stubbornly refused to recognize British control and occupied Tobago twice in the late 1700s and early 1800s. But the British finally regained Tobago, until its Independence in 1962.

During this time, Trinidad was still ruled by the Spanish, but they could not persuade their own people to settle on the island. In 1776 Roman Catholic Frenchmen were invited to immigrate from Haiti, St. Lucia, and Martinique. The influx of Frenchmen—along with their African slaves—caused the population of Trinidad to multiply tenfold between 1760 and 1787. As one historian described the island, Trinidad was a Spanish colony ruled by Frenchmen.

The French introduced the use of herbs and spices, which are hallmarks of T&T cookery today. Creole chives, the Spanish or broadleaf thyme, French or fine thyme, aniseed, and basil were grown in small family plots, along with garlic and onions. Today, in high mountain villages outside of Maraval, such as Paramin, these herbs are still grown on steep mountainsides, which ensures good drainage. The herb and vegetable growers of the region were immortalized in song by The Tiger (Neville Marcano) in 1937:

> I want a girl born in Maraval
> Because she ain't adoring Carnival.
> She could plant balangen, chive, an' coffee
> So I can live independently.

The French settlers also introduced black pudding, a highly spiced blood sausage, and souse, pig's feet or seafood marinated in lime juice, hot chile peppers, onion, and cucumbers. Recipes for both of these dishes are found in Chapter 7.

Trinidadian planters realized that it was cheaper to allow the slaves to feed themselves rather than to buy imported foods for them, so the slaves were provided certain areas that they could cultivate. They grew peas, plantains, pumpkins, *dasheen* (taro), corn, and numerous fruits. Peas, which became a staple of life, were brought from Africa, and the dish called peas and rice lives on today in Trinidadian cuisine. Indeed, nearly every island in the Caribbean has its own variation of this dish. Trinidadian cooks prefer to cook the dish with pigeon peas (and sometimes black-eyed peas as opposed to the kidney beans used in the Jamaican version of the dish), and they are found often in *pelau* (page 60). Interestingly enough, peanuts (called groundnuts) never caught on in T&T as they did on the other Caribbean islands.

Hot chile peppers were commonly used by the slaves to season most dishes. Gertrude Carmichael, who lived in Trinidad in the early 1700s, wrote: "Capsicums—his seasoning for all dishes—they are never wanting.... Every variety of *capsicum* is to be found on a West Indian estate; indeed, they are almost a weed."

Slave dishes that live on today include *sancoche,* a vegetable and meat stew, and *coo-coo,* a cornmeal pudding with okra, which was cooked in a simple pot over coals. Ground provisions such as *dasheen* provided the elephant-ear-sized leaves for callaloo, a soup made with okra and coconut milk that Trinidad calls its own, but it is also prepared on many other West Indian islands. It often contains crab meat or lobster.

In order to utilize all the available food, the slaves also became talented fishermen, using canoes fashioned from logs with adzes to catch kingfish, barracudas, groupers, and sharks. Today fishermen still ply the waters beyond the surf at Maracas Bay for sharks, the steaks of which are served up at beach shacks as the famous shark-and-bake (page 70). In the waters off Tobago, flying fish are caught by spreading palm fronds over the surface of the water. The fish, deceived into thinking that the fronds are the beach where they can lay their eggs, leap onto the fronds and are captured. The fillets are usually deep-fried, but they can also be stewed. Other popular seafoods are conch, land crabs, lobster, and oysters.

The slaves were often given sugar and molasses as bonuses, from which they created many candies and desserts. Two notable sugar-based desserts that live on from slave days are *toolum* (page 92), which is made with molasses and coconut, and sugar cake, which combines sugar with grated coconut.

With the efforts of the French planters and their slave labor, Trinidad became one of the wealthiest islands in the West Indies. By 1797 there were 468 plantations; 159 of them were growing sugar cane on a total of 86,000 acres. Trinidad was ripe for the plucking.

And plucked it was in 1797, when the British fleet, on its way to attack Puerto Rico, captured Trinidad without firing a shot. Totally outmanned, the Spanish navy—consisting of a mere five ships—was scuttled in Chaguaramas Bay by its commander. The conquering of Trinidad was rather late, considering the fact that the British had occupied Barbados since the early 1600s and Jamaica since 1655.

One of the more notable British food introductions to Trinidad was the breadfruit. William Bligh, the infamous captain of the *Bounty*, had brought breadfruit to St. Vincent from Tahiti in 1793, and soon after the British "conquered" Trinidad, the tree was imported there. According to legend, every slave family in Trinidad was given a breadfruit tree to feed them in case of a crop failure. Breadfruit was commonly combined with coconut milk to make the delicious dish called breadfruit oil-down (page 87).

The British also introduced the tamarind from the East Indies, which was used to make sauces such as the famous Worcestershire. The British also brought to Trinidad turnips and cabbage, two common vegetables in T&T markets today. They enjoyed local game such as Muscovy duck as well as imported meats such as chicken, pork, and beef, which were usually roasted or stewed. The British were also responsible for the popularity of fruit jellies and marmalades, which are still produced in great quantities in T&T.

Today, with all the ethnic influences on T&T cuisine, distinctions are made to keep those various influences somewhat separate. East Indian and Chinese foods are considered distinct, and the remainder of the cooking is usually lumped together in the category of Creole. But Creole cooking in the T&T sense has nothing to do with New Orleans. The term was first used to describe Europeans born in the New World, but today it means a person of mixed European and African descent. Thus Creole cooking is considered native, a reference to the earlier inhabitants of T&T as opposed to the later East Indians and Chinese.

Noted Creole chef Jean de Boissiere advised in 1948: "As all Creole cooking is international, all national prejudices must be dropped and our food approached with an open palate." The cooking style is characterized by the use of hot chile peppers, salted butter, garlic, onions, and many spices. Most of the dishes in the recipe chapters of this book are considered to be Creole.

East Indian, West Indian

In 1834 slavery was abolished in Trinidad and Tobago, which profoundly affected the food history of the two islands. In 1838 in Trinidad, the mandatory four-year apprenticeship ended and some 20,000 slaves who worked the enormous sugar cane plantations left the estates and became squatters. This resulted in an enormous labor shortage.

The shortage was filled by freed slaves from other islands, plus a huge influx of laborers from India and Pakistan. Beginning in 1845, a mass migration of workers from those two countries over the next seventy-two years increased the population of Trinidad by 145,000. The laborers were indentured, and each immigrant agreed to work for five years in return for five acres of land. By the 1940s, the East Indian influence was so prevalent that travel writer Patrick Leigh Fermor wrote: "Wide tracts of Trinidad are now, for all visual purposes, Bengal."

Because the East Indians were thrown together in a strange land and were forced to share tasks equally, divisions of caste and religion were soon dissolved. But unlike the Africans before them, the East Indian immigrants were allowed to keep their language, clothing, and food. Two animals that immigrated with them were the water buffalo—useful for heavy labor—and the white humped cattle, which provided the milk for both the beloved yogurt and the butter, which was made into ghee (clarified butter).

Many East Indian foods and cooking techniques were introduced into T&T, notably curries and rice (rice is still grown on Trinidad today). Most of the curries made today are much milder than those of India because the cooks lack ground hot chile peppers (most of the chile peppers are used fresh and are not sold in the dried form). However, hot pepper sauces are often added to curried dishes at the table. Some cooks still use old-fashioned curry pastes, which usually have hot chile peppers added to them.

Every imaginable foodstuff is curried, including mangos, pumpkins, eggplant, potatoes, green tomatoes, okra, chicken, fish, beef, pork, goat, and lamb. Two major brands of commercial curry powder available on the islands, Chief's and Turban, battle it out for consumer loyalty; a typical commercial mixture usually contains varying amounts of coriander, cumin, turmeric, fenugreek, celery seed, and fennel.

Sophisticated citizens who have traveled outside the country realize that there is more to curry than just the T&T style, but any changes are unlikely. One restaurant owner told us she was disappointed when Gaylord's, a restaurant on Independence Square that served authentic East Indian curries, failed because the locals said: "This isn't curry." Noted food writer Julie Sahni believes that "curry is such an integral part of Trinidadian cuisine that its Indian origin is actually being lost." She was amazed when a Trinidadian saleswoman in a curry factory asked her: "Are you from India? Do they have curry powder in India?"

Breads are one of the hallmarks of the East Indian influence on West Indian cooking. One local T&T cookbook has seven recipes for various types of East Indian breads, including *bara*, *chapatti*, *nan*, *dhalpurie*, and three different types of *roti* bread. Some, such as *bara*, are fried in oil, but most are cooked on griddles (*tawas*) or baking stones and are very thin. Cooks lacking a griddle can use a large heavy cast-iron skillet. Fritterlike breads, especially those using split peas, are also popular. *Phulouri*, *kachouri*, and *saheena* (the spellings of these may vary) have split pea flour combined with spices such as turmeric and are fried in oil. *Saheena* contains *dasheen* leaves, garlic, and hot chile peppers and makes a particularly tasty fritter snack or appetizer.

Everywhere in T&T are food stands or small restaurants selling *roti*, which the citizens proudly claim as unique to the two islands. Although *roti* is a generic term for *chapatti*-like breads in India, the technique of wrapping *roti* bread around curried stuffings seems to have originated in Trinidad. The burrito-like sandwich that results is generically called *roti* and is beloved in T&T.

One of the more popular *roti* restaurants, Patraj, in San Juan, offers nine different kinds of *roti*: chicken, fish, liver, goat, beef, conch, shrimp, duck, and potato *channa* in two different styles. The curried filling is either wrapped in *roti* bread or served with torn-up bread, which is dipped into the fillings. The latter bread is called "buss-up-shut," a corruption of "burst up shirt," since the bread resembles torn cloth. Some practice is required to eat it gracefully.

Roti has been described as "Trinidad's main contribution to world cuisine" by calypso writer Daisann McLane, who says that it is a "thoroughly Creole invention that has no equivalent in India."

McLane's expansion of the term "Creole" to include West Indian variations on East Indian foods was applauded by food historian Raymond Sokolov. "This observation succinctly raises the complex issue of what Creole means," he wrote. "The term is meaningless if it does not refer to a New World culture that evolved amidst a transplanted Old World population. In this sense, the Trinidadian *roti* is a perfect creolism, since it evolved directly and obviously from Asian Indian foodways."

American observers may believe that Creole food in T&T now includes *roti*, but from our observations in the country, the Trinis do not. Creole restaurants are distinctly different from *roti* shops, and the two cooking styles are rarely combined in a single establishment. Also, in Jean de Boissiere's classic 1948 cookbook, *Cooking Creole*, he does not even mention *roti*, although he does include recipes for curried shrimp and curried mutton. The debate about the definition of Creole cooking will probably never be resolved.

Another popular T&T food sold at roadside stands is "doubles." This simple dish features a sandwich of two pieces of fried *bara* bread with several fillings: usually curried chick-peas, a hot sauce, and *kucheela*, a spicy mango pickle. Gathered around a typical doubles stand at any given time will be people from all economic strata—from a businessman in shirt and tie to a field worker.

More Immigrants

The East Indians were not the only indentured immigrants to influence the cuisine of T&T. Portuguese and Chinese workers were also encouraged to immigrate after slavery was abolished. In 1846 the first Portuguese workers arrived from Madeira to work on the cocoa plantations. They were a part of the 40,000 workers who would eventually settle in Trinidad, Guyana, and, to a lesser extent, in Jamaica and Grenada. Life was rather harsh for these settlers, and some sources estimate that only one-third of them survived to marry and have children.

Although the Portuguese did not influence the cuisine as much as the East Indians did, they brought food traditions that linger to this day in T&T. A seafaring people, the Portuguese brought salt cod (called *bacalao*) with them, which still plays an important role in the local cuisine. The cod is soaked first, then can be grilled, sautéed in olive oil, or flaked and fried with tomatoes and other vegetables. It is also a primary ingredient in *buljol*, a kind of fish salad with lime, and *accras*, a fish dumpling. *Piri piri*, a hot chile pepper oil, is a Portuguese specialty that is often served with fish.

The Portuguese loved marinated meats; two popular entrees served today are marinated hare and garlic pork. The hare, or *lapp* as it's called in T&T, is marinated in a combination of rum, wine, and spices. A similar recipe is used for the wild agouti, a large, rabbitlike animal that is commonly hunted in T&T.

Garlic pork, a Christmas tradition in both T&T and Guyana, features either a pork roast or spareribs marinated in vinegar and lime juice heavily infused with garlic. One recipe in a local cookbook calls for marinating the pork in the refrigerator for six weeks! A week is usually long enough.

The Chinese also influenced the culture and food of T&T. The main influence evident today is the use of fresh ginger, soy sauce, and honey. In 1854 the first two boatloads of immigrants from China arrived in Trinidad, Jamaica, and Guyana. Because of the Chinese tradition of binding the feet of women, women were unwelcome on the plantations, so the men outnumbered them by twenty-five to one. The Chinese adapted well to sugar cane growing and were considered the best plantation workers.

Because the Chinese were reluctant to use the native foods of other ethnic groups and disliked such staples as coconut milk, the early Trinidadian-Chinese kitchen was limited to dishes such as chow mein, chop suey, *pow* dumplings, and various pickles. By the late 1800s, however, dried noodles, soy sauce, and five-spice powder became available. And as the Chinese moved off the plantations and formed their own communities—after the practice of reindenturing the immigrants was discontinued in the 1870s—they planted crops such as bok choy, ginger, Chinese parsley (coriander or cilantro), and beans. Other Chinese opened retail shops and moved strongly into the world of commerce. Interestingly enough, despite their supposed disdain for local cooking, some Chinese opened stands and restaurants that served East Indian and Creole food. As early as 1910, the calypsonian Mighty Growler was singing:

> A man in suit, a tie, and waist coat
> Ask the Chinese man to trust him accra and float.
> "Me no trust um," bawl out the Chinese man.
> "And you better move back from my frying pan!"

The food history of T&T did not change much in the late nineteenth and early twentieth century. In

Tobago the sugar industry collapsed, and the planters turned to coconut and cocoa. In 1889 Tobago joined with Trinidad to become a single British colony, in which the sugar industry expanded. The discovery of petroleum resources in 1908 further brightened T&T's economic future. In fact, by 1935, Atilla the Hun and Lord Beginner were singing:

How different is the island we know
To the Trinidad of long ago.
She's really the gem of the Antilles
An' the queen of the West Indies.
With motor-cars runnin' up and down
Trinidad comin' like-a New York town.

Despite such optimism induced by oil revenues, T&T could not avoid the effects of the Depression. In 1935 The Tiger portrayed that Trinis were worse off than dogs:

A dog can walk about and take up bone
Fowl head, stale bread, fish tail, and pone.
If it's a good breed and not too wild
Some people will take it an' mind it like a child.
But when a hungry man goes out to beg
They will set a bulldog behind his leg.
Forty policemen may chalk him down too
You see where a dog is better than you.

The Depression forced many Trinis to economize by preparing the less expensive East Indian fare, which they still regarded disparagingly as "coolie" cooking. In 1936 The Lion's calypso "Bargee Pelauri" contained some fascinating insights into T&T cookery of the time and described how East Indian cooking became popular with the Creole population:

Though depression is in Trinidad
Maintaining a wife isn't very hard.
Well, you need no ham nor biscuit nor bread
But there are some ways that they can easily be fed.
Like the coolies, on bargee pelauri
Dhalpat and dalpouri
Channa parata and the aloo in talkaree.
I want you young men to realize
That these are the days to economize.
Though your wife may need your crab an' the callaloo
Stew beef or pork an pound plantain too.
But the time is too hard to get that today
An' so you got to feed the wife the easiest way.
Like the coolies, on bargee pelauri
Dhalpat and dalpouri
Channa parata and the aloo in talkaree.
Though depression is in Trinidad
Maintaining a wife isn't very hard.

The American Fast Food Invasion

On August 31, 1962, T&T gained its independence from Britain but were about to be invaded by another power—American fast foods. In 1968 fast food arrived in Port of Spain with the opening of the first Royal Castle, a "take-away" restaurant specializing in chicken and chips. The chain was started by Vernon and Irene Montrichard and Marie and Ray Permenter, who had a unique selling proposition. The chicken and fish served at the Royal Castles were marinated in a hot pepper sauce containing herbs, ginger, and garlic. The recipe proved to be a hit: The Royal Castle sauce became famous, and the future seemed secure for the home-grown fast food.

Then in the mid-1970s Kentucky Fried Chicken took T&T by storm with fifteen locations; abundant radio, TV, and newspaper advertising; and a delivery service. One location, on Independence Square, was reputedly the highest grossing KFC location in the world, doing US$200,000 a day during Carnival. KFC bought the rights to use *soca* singer Arrow's song "Hot, Hot, Hot" to promote their Hot Wings.

Royal Castle fought back: It hired an advertising agency, began to sponsor concerts, and ran radio and TV ads. Sales doubled at the Royal Castles, and soon there were thirteen locations—evidence that the people of T&T are crazy about chicken.

They also love the locally grown hot chile peppers, called Congo peppers or simply hot peppers, which are a variety of the species *Capsicum chinense*. (Similar peppers of this species are called Habanero and Scotch bonnet in other parts of the Caribbean.) A milder chile pepper called pimiento or seasoning pepper is also grown, as are bell peppers, but most of the acreage in T&T is devoted to the Congo pepper. Approximately 2,000 acres of Congo peppers are under cultivation in T&T and much of this crop is exported. The total exports to Canada, the United States, and the United Kingdom amounted to TT$1.6 million in 1991, with about 131 tons alone exported to the United States, mostly in mash form.

The rest of the crop is sold in local markets and used in commercial hot sauces. Although every family in T&T seems to have its own recipe, the homemade sauces have not prevented a large hot sauce industry from springing up. There are five major manufacturers of hot sauce in T&T and about ten minor ones. The best-known T&T hot sauces available in the United States are the Matouks' hot sauces and the Royal Castle herb-infused green hot sauce, which is marketed as Trinidad Pepper Sauce. The Matouks' brand—a blend of papaya, peppers, and spices—is available in three heat levels. About half of their sauce production is consumed locally; the rest is exported, mostly to the United States and Canada.

In current Trini slang, *makaforshet* means "leftovers." We hope you have plenty of *makaforshet* left after cooking with our collection of T&T recipes. But when guests are about, don't forget the warning of Wilmoth Houdini in his 1932 calypso:

> After Johnnie eat my food
> After Johnnie wear my clothes
> After Johnnie drink my rum
> Johnnie turn around an' he take my wife!

shadow bennie:
sauces, seasonings,
and condiments

It is appropriate that the first recipes in this book are infused with herbs because fresh herbs play a significant role in the cuisine of T&T. We were introduced to the herb called Shadow Bennie at Maracas Bay, when a sauce thick with it was poured over fried shark. The flavor was vaguely familiar, but no one seemed able to tell us any other common name for the herb, much less the botanical name. The name Shadow Bennie seems to be derived from the words *chadon bene*, but we have been unable to find their origin in either French or Spanish. The name is probably *patois*, roughly meaning "good tea," since the leaves are boiled, and the tea is consumed as a folk remedy for pneumonia, flu, constipation, diabetes, and malaria. The roots are eaten as a cure for scorpion stings; fortunately we didn't have occasion to test the effectiveness of that remedy.

On a trip to the market in Scarborough, Tobago, we asked our guide to find Shadow Bennie for us, so we could identify it from the leaves. Basil Phillips walked around the market and finally located some. It turned out to be the herb known in Spanish as culantro (*Eryngium foetidum*). We find that cilantro is a good substitute.

We were fortunate enough to visit the herb fields of Paramin, outside Maraval. There on the steep slopes, where it rains every day during the wet season, farmers grow numerous herbs that are sold in the Central Market on Beetham Road in Port of Spain. We met herb growers Duffy and Kimoy Lamy, who grow Spanish thyme, French thyme, chives, and basil. Spanish thyme is also known as Indian borage (*Coleus amboinicus*) and Cuban oregano; its origin is unknown. A broadleaf succulent, it is grown as a fresh herb in many parts of the Caribbean. A good substitute is a combination of French thyme and Greek oregano. Chives grown in Trinidad have a different flavor and aroma than American-grown chives. Fresh shallots are a good substitute.

The herbs grown at Paramin are often made into seasoning mixtures, or pastes, for marinating meat or flavoring stews and casseroles. We have included recipes for several variations of these seasoning mixtures.

The Lamys were kind enough to describe their herb-growing techniques and to give us a remedy for indigestion, which is a tea made from basil, aniseed, and mint (page 46).

We also toured the Congo pepper-growing operation of Marie Permenter and Vernon Montrichard near Oropuche in Trinidad, where we saw fields with plants four to five feet tall, some bearing hundreds of pods. ("Congo" means large in Trini slang.) The Congo peppers are extremely hot and aromatic and are commonly made into sauces. We have included several different versions to give the cook an idea of how varied the sauces are in T&T.

Another commonly used condiment is curry. Because of the large East Indian population in T&T, curries have become very popular in the country, and they are most commonly served in *roti* shops. "Without access to their curry," wrote calypso writer Daisann McLane, "Trinidadian cooks would be as lost as Sicilians without fresh garlic."

There are several incarnations of curry. *Masalas* are the mildest spice blends, usually made without chili powder or turmeric. *Masalas* are added to cooked meats and vegetables. *Garam masala* literally means "hot spices." *Amchar masala*, a blend of coriander, fenugreek, fennel, mustard, and cumin, is commonly used to season cooked green mangoes. (*Amchar* is the Hindi word for mango.)

Commercial curry powders, such as the Raja Jahan brand, contain coriander, cumin, turmeric, fenugreek, celery seed, fennel, and *mangril*, a mystery ingredient variously identified by the locals as curry leaf or poppy seeds. Most likely, the word is a corruption of the Hindi word *mangrail*, which is onion seed.

Other popular commercial curry powders are Turban, Chief (which contains black pepper), and Indi, a Guyanese brand containing some hot chile peppers. Tunapuna, a town about halfway between Port of Spain and Arima, is the curry powder capital of Trinidad, as described by Daisann McLane: "Clouds of roasted cumin and turmeric, garlic, coriander, and those acidly hot Caribbean peppers . . . simply by breathing, one was exposed to hazardous levels of piquant longing."

Most of the curries served in Trinidad are not particularly fiery—until a Congo pepper sauce is added at the table. But some curries, such as the curry pastes, contain various amounts of crushed Congo peppers. We have included two versions of prepared curry mixtures—a *masala* and a curry paste—so cooks can select their own heat level.

Chutneys are also extremely popular in T&T, and there are literally dozens of recipes. We have chosen some of the best-tasting ones for this chapter.

Incidentally, coconut milk and cream are important ingredients in many T&T recipes. You can purchase canned coconut milk or use the recipe that is provided (page 36). Canned coconut cream is not recommended, since it is excessively sweet.

Shadow Bennie Sauce

This is the sauce that is served over Shark-and-Bake (page 70) at Maracas Bay—a presentation that is similar to malt vinegar served over fish and chips in England. The sauce can be spiced up by increasing the amount of Congo peppers in the recipe.

1/4 cup minced Shadow Bennie (culantro)
   or cilantro
3/4 cup white wine vinegar
1 clove garlic, minced
1 teaspoon vegetable oil
1/4 teaspoon minced Congo peppers or
   Habaneros

Combine all of the ingredients in a jar and allow to stand for at least 2 hours at room temperature for the flavors to blend. The sauce will keep indefinitely in the refrigerator.

Yield: Makes about 1 cup.

Joe's Shadow Bennie Sauce

Here is a variation of the basic Shadow Bennie herbal sauce. When we asked Joe Brown of the Solimar Restaurant how he creates new dishes, he said: "It is important to marry the best of everything to bring out the natural flavors." He went on to state that if you start with top-notch ingredients, you can produce noteworthy food. All of the herbs used at the Solimar come from Joe's personal herb garden.

1/2 cup coarsely chopped Shadow Bennie
   (culantro) or cilantro
2 teaspoons small-leaf fresh basil or
   1 teaspoon dried basil
2 teaspoons fresh thyme or
   1 teaspoon dried thyme
1/4 cup chopped fresh parsley
1 clove garlic, minced
1/4 Congo pepper or Habanero, seeds and
   stem removed, minced
1/2 cup freshly squeezed lime juice

Combine all of the ingredients and let the mixture stand for at least an hour at room temperature for the flavors to blend. The sauce will keep indefinitely in the refrigerator.

Yield: Makes about 1 cup.

Moko Jumbie Creole Pepper Sauce

Named after the zombie-like stilt character that prowls around during Carnival celebrations, this sauce features two ingredients common to Trinidadian commercial sauces—fresh papaya and dried mustard. The sauce can be used as a condiment or as a marinade for meat, poultry, and fish.

1 small green papaya
8 cups water
5 Congo peppers or Habaneros, seeds and stems removed, chopped
1 large onion, finely chopped
2 cloves garlic, minced
4 tablespoons dried mustard
2 tablespoons salt (or less, to taste)
3 cups distilled white vinegar (or 1 1/2 cups vinegar mixed with 1 1/2 cups water)
1/2 teaspoon ground turmeric
1 teaspoon Trinidadian Curry Paste (page 35)

Boil the papaya (in its skin) in the 8 cups of water for 10 minutes, then remove from the water and let cool. Peel the papaya and remove the seeds; chop flesh into 1-inch cubes.

In a large saucepan combine the papaya with the remaining ingredients. Bring to a boil, then reduce heat and simmer for 20 minutes.

Remove from the heat and let cool, then purée in a food processor and transfer to sterilized bottles or jars. The sauce will last for weeks in the refrigerator.

Yield: Makes 3 to 4 cups.

Tiki Village Congo Pepper Sauce

At our first lunch in T&T, Diana Cohen-Chan, manager of the Kapok Hotel, treated us to a dim sum feast with a difference at her top-floor restaurant. The difference was revealed as Ramesh Ghany (a chef of East Indian descent cooking at a Chinese restaurant) told us how he makes his simple Creole Congo pepper sauce. Since Ramesh uses 300 Congo peppers to make a gallon of sauce, we've scaled down the recipe to more modest dimensions.

3/4 cup vegetable oil
20 large Congo peppers or Habaneros, seeds and stems removed, very finely minced or puréed in a food processor

In a large saucepan bring the oil to a boil. Add the peppers, then turn off the heat and allow the mixture to stand for at least 30 minutes before using. Store in a sterilized jar in the refrigerator.

Yield: Makes about 1 cup.

Johnny's Food Haven Pepper Sauce

The motto at Johnny's Food Haven is "Trinidad home cooking away from home." Johnny serves his food cafeteria-style—one of only two or three restaurants to do so in Trinidad. Ladies take note: As of this writing, Johnny is thirty-one years old, single, and an expert cook. This sauce is extremely hot. To make it milder, add cooked pumpkin or cooked finely grated carrot.

5 Congo peppers or Habaneros (or as many
  peppers as can be stuffed into a 1-cup
  measure)
1 cup water
1/2 teaspoon salt
1 onion, minced
2 cloves garlic, minced
1/4 cup minced Shadow Bennie (*culantro*)
  or cilantro

    Purée the peppers with the water in a blender. Add the remaining ingredients and let stand for at least 1 hour for flavors to blend. Serve with grilled meats, poultry, or fish.

Yield: Makes about 2 cups.

Bird Peppers in Sherry

This recipe, which we found in a 1940s Trinidad cookbook, is probably one of the earliest methods of preserving hot chile peppers in the tropics. It is also called pepper wine. The sherry, which gradually picks up heat from the bird peppers, is sprinkled into soups and stews and makes them taste quite exotic. The peppers can be either fresh or dried.

20 bird peppers (*chiltepins*), stems
  removed
1 cup dry sherry

    Add the peppers to the sherry and allow to steep for several days at room temperature or in the refrigerator. Store in a sterilized jar in the refrigerator.

Yield: Makes about 1 cup.

Creole Pickle

This old recipe creates both pickles and a vinegar sauce, which can be sprinkled on just about any dish to add flavor and heat. When stored in a sterilized jar in the refrigerator, it will last for years.

1 quart distilled white vinegar
1 clove garlic, crushed
5 seasoning peppers or Yellow Wax Hots, seeds and stems removed
2 Congo peppers or Habaneros, seeds and stems removed, quartered
2 cups diced green papaya that has been parboiled for 2 minutes
4 small onions, quartered

In a large saucepan bring the vinegar and garlic to a boil; let boil for 5 minutes. Remove from the heat and allow to cool to room temperature.

Cut the seasoning peppers into chunks the same size as the quartered Congo peppers. Distribute equal portions of pepper pieces, papaya, and onions in six 1-cup sterilized jars. Add vinegar to cover contents and seal jars. Allow to stand for at least 2 weeks before using.

Yield: Makes about 6 cups.

Solimar Sweet and Sour Chile Dip

This sauce can be used in place of barbecue sauce for grilling meats, or as a dip for plantain chips and other snacks.

6 tablespoons barbecue sauce
6 tablespoons catsup
1/2 Congo pepper or Habanero, seeds and stem removed, minced
2 tablespoons vinegar, preferably pepper vinegar
2 tablespoons minced dill pickle
1 clove garlic, crushed
1/4 teaspoon freshly ground black pepper

Combine all of the ingredients and let stand at room temperature for at least 1 hour for flavors to blend. Store in a sterilized jar in the refrigerator.

Yield: About 1 cup.

West Indian Masala

This spice blend is superior to commercial *masalas* because the freshly ground seeds have not oxidized and lost their flavor. Generally speaking, when turmeric is added to *masala,* it becomes curry powder.

6 tablespoons coriander seeds
1 teaspoon fenugreek seeds
2 teaspoons fennel seeds
1 teaspoon mustard seeds
1 1/2 teaspoons cumin seeds
2 teaspoons ground turmeric (optional)

Roast all the seeds in a large pan in a 350 degree F oven until the seeds begin to pop. Place a baking sheet on top of the pan and roast for an additional 8 minutes, taking care not to burn the seeds.

Let the seeds cool, then finely grind them together in a spice grinder or with a mortar and pestle. If you wish to make a curry powder, add turmeric and mix well. Store in an airtight container.

Yield: Makes about 1/2 cup.

Trinidadian Curry Paste

Many Trinidadian curry powders lack hot chile peppers; instead, hot sauces are placed on the table when a meal is served. This recipe, however, found in an early Trinidad cookbook, does call for hot chile peppers. The paste can be used in recipes calling for *masala* or curry powder.

6 tablespoons roasted coriander seeds
1 teaspoon roasted aniseeds
1 teaspoon roasted whole cloves
1 teaspoon ground turmeric
1 teaspoon roasted cumin seeds
1 teaspoon roasted fenugreek seeds
1 teaspoon roasted black peppercorns
1 teaspoon roasted mustard seeds
2 cloves garlic, chopped
1 large onion, chopped
1/2 Congo pepper or Habanero, seeds and
   stem removed, chopped
Water, as needed

Grind all of the ingredients into a paste with a mortar and pestle, or purée in a food processor. Store in a sterilized jar in the refrigerator.

Yield: Makes 1 1/2 to 2 cups.

All-Purpose Seasoning Mixture

This seasoning sauce, which can also be used as a marinade (see Note), adds considerable liveliness to otherwise bland grilled lamb, pork chops, or chicken. Or try it as a basting sauce for grilled vegetables, such as eggplant and zucchini. Some of the measurements are authentically vague, so experiment with the amounts that please you. Note that chives in Trinidad have a different flavor and aroma than American-grown chives. Fresh shallots are a good substitute.

3 bunches Trinidad chives, green onions,
   or shallots, coarsely chopped
1 bunch parsley, coarsely chopped
1/2 bunch celery leaves, coarsely chopped
1 cup peeled garlic cloves
1 tablespoon minced Congo pepper or
   Habanero
1 leaf Spanish thyme *or* 1 teaspoon fresh
French thyme and 1/2 teaspoon fresh
   Greek oregano
1 tablespoon fresh or dried French thyme
1/2 cup distilled white vinegar
1 tablespoon salt (or less, to taste)
1 tablespoon ground ginger

Combine all of the ingredients in a food processor and blend thoroughly. Store in sterilized jars in the refrigerator.

Yield: Makes 2 to 3 cups.

Note: When using this sauce as a meat marinade, combine 3 tablespoons of the mixture with 1/2 teaspoon soy sauce, ground black pepper to taste, 1/2 cup chopped tomatoes, and 1 teaspoon Worcestershire sauce. This is enough to marinate 1 1/2 pounds of meat. Marinate in the refrigerator, preferably overnight or for at least 2 to 3 hours.

Nancy's Seasoning Paste

This basic condiment is used to marinate chicken. T&T cook Nancy Ramesar adds a dash of it to all her East Indian dishes.

12 cloves garlic, chopped
8 medium onions, chopped
6 seasoning peppers or Yellow Wax Hots,
   seeds and stems removed, chopped
1 teaspoon dried thyme or sage (optional)

    Purée all of the ingredients in a blender. Transfer the mixture to a large sterilized jar and refrigerate until needed.

Yield: Makes about 3 cups.

Paramin Herb Seasoning

Inspired by the mountaintop herb fields of Paramin, this seasoning can be used as a marinade for fish and poultry, or as a tasty addition to salad dressings, sauces, and dips. In Trinidad, the recipe would call for Spanish thyme and the large native chives, but we have made appropriate stateside substitutions. The seasoning mix will last for about a month in the refrigerator.

4 large shallots, chopped
1 bunch green onions or chives, chopped
1/4 cup minced fresh thyme
1/4 cup chopped fresh parsely
1 tablespoon minced Shadow Bennie
   (*culantro*) or cilantro
1 large onion, chopped
3 cloves garlic, minced
1/2 teaspoon freshly ground black pepper
1/2 teaspoon salt
2 tablespoons distilled white vinegar
Water, as needed

    Grind all of the ingredients together with a mortar and pestle, or purée in a food processor. The mixture should be slightly liquid, so add water as necessary for consistency.

Yield: Makes 2 1/2 to 3 cups.

Coconut Milk and Cream

Both of these liquids are extracts from coconut. It is important to differentiate them from the sweetened, canned coconut cream (or syrup), which is used to make drinks called piña coladas. The canned cream is not a substitute and should not be used in any recipe in this book. Coconut milk is used extensively in sauces, stews, and curries. It is best made from freshly grated coconut meat, but if that is not available, use dessicated, unsweetened coconut flakes and substitute cow's milk for the water. For milk that is almost the thickness of cream, instead of steeping coconut in hot water, purée in a blender and then strain through cloth.

4 cups grated coconut
2 cups boiling water or hot milk

    In a large bowl cover the grated coconut with the boiling water and let steep for 15 minutes.
    Drain the coconut through a strainer, reserving liquid ("milk"). The coconut meat may be squeezed through muslin cloth to collect the remaining liquid.
    Store the coconut milk in the refrigerator (it has about the same shelf life as whole milk); the "cream" will rise to the top.

Yield: Makes about 2 cups.

Mango Kucheela

This relish is commonly served with curried dishes of all types, as well as with *pelau* (page 60). Note that the mangoes should be green; ripe mangoes are never used in *kucheela*.

2 cups grated flesh of green mangoes
4 cloves garlic, minced
2 Congo peppers or Habaneros, seeds and
   stems removed, minced
2 teaspoons West Indian Masala (page 34)
1/2 cup mustard oil or vegetable oil, or
   more for texture

Squeeze as much juice as possible from the grated mango, then spread on a baking sheet, place in a 250 degree F oven, and cook until dried (about 2 hours).

Combine with the remaining ingredients and mix well, adding enough mustard oil to make a slightly soupy consistency. Store in sterilized jars in the refrigerator.

Yield: Makes about 2 cups.

Ramesar Mango Chutney

This chutney, served to us by Nancy Ramesar, is the simplest recipe we found for this condiment. It makes a delicious dip for plantain chips, *phulouri*, or crackers. It's best when used within a half hour of making, but the addition of 1/4 teaspoon lime juice will preserve it.

1 half-ripe mango, peeled and seeded
4 cloves garlic
1 Congo pepper or Habanero, seeds and
   stem removed, chopped
Pinch sugar

Combine all of the ingredients in a blender and purée until smooth.

Yield: Makes about 1 cup.

Marie's Green Mango Chutney

One evening at Marie Permenter's house, with Scotch and coconut water cocktails in hand, we started discussing the versatility of mangoes. Marie dashed into the kitchen and proceeded to whip up the following chutney for us to taste. Although we expected the flavor to be overwhelming based on the ingredients, it was actually delicate. The chutney is good used as a dip for chips (plantain chips work well), vegetables, or crackers.

1 head garlic, peeled and puréed in a
   blender
4 green mangoes, peeled, pits removed,
   and coarsely diced
1 tablespoon sugar
Dash salt
4 leaves Shadow Bennie (*culantro*)
   or 1/4 cup chopped cilantro
1 leaf Spanish thyme *or* 1 teaspoon fresh
   French thyme and 1/2 teaspoon fresh
   Greek oregano

To the garlic in the blender add the remaining ingredients; blend until the mixture is very fine and almost runny. Serve immediately or cover and refrigerate for later use. Bring to room temperature before serving.

Yield: Makes 1 1/2 to 2 cups.

Tamarind Mango Chutney

This exotic relish with the flavor of the islands is served with grilled meats, seafood, and curried dishes.

1 1/2 cups distilled white vinegar
1 cup firmly packed brown sugar
1 1/2 cups minced green mango
1/8 cup grated fresh ginger
3 medium onions, minced
1 Congo pepper or Habanero, seeds and
    stem removed, minced (optional)
1 clove garlic, minced
1 teaspoon salt
1/2 cup raisins, minced
1/2 cup tamarind juice (see Note)

In a large saucepan over medium heat, bring the vinegar to a boil; add the brown sugar and cook until the sugar dissolves. Add the mango, ginger, onions, Congo pepper, and garlic. Reduce the heat to low and cook until the mango is soft.

Add the salt, raisins, and tamarind juice; continue cooking until the mixture reaches the consistency of marmalade. Bottle in sterilized jars.

Yield: Makes 3 cups.

Note: Tamarind juice is available in Asian markets. The juice can also be made from dried pods by removing the seeds and dried pulp, boiling them with water, and then straining the liquid through muslin.

Papaya Chutney with Raisins

This chutney features another island favorite, *pawpaw*, or papaya, which is available at roadside fruit stands. We bought several ripe ones at the stand outside the Kapok Hotel and ate them with lime juice squeezed over them. Don't try this with green papaya called for in this recipe.

2 cups grated green papaya
1 tablespoon grated fresh ginger
3 tablespoons grated lime zest
1 teaspoon salt
1/2 Congo pepper or Habanero, seeds and
    stem removed, minced
1 clove garlic, minced
1/2 cup sugar
1/4 cup grated onion
1/4 cup distilled white vinegar
1/2 cup water
1/2 cup minced raisins

In a large saucepan over medium heat, combine all of the ingredients except the raisins. Bring to a boil, then reduce the heat to low and simmer, stirring occasionally, until the mixture starts to thicken (about 15 minutes). Add the raisins and cook until the mixture is quite thick. Store in sterilized jars in the refrigerator.

Yield: Makes about 3 cups.

doubles:
drinks and appetizers

In T&T, "doubles" means both double-sized drinks and doubled-up snacks, such as two pieces of *bara* bread sandwiching *channa*, hot sauce, and *kucheela*. There are two types of *bara*, one made with split pea flour and baking powder and the other made with wheat flour and yeast. Since there is a choice of breads and some variety in the fillings, debates rage over which vendor has the best doubles in Port of Spain.

After a television appearance, advertising businessmen Michael Coehlo and Keith Nexar took us to their favorite doubles vendor. On the way we invented ad slogans for selling these treats. Michael's favorite was "What I would give for a single double." We came up with "Doubles are singled out as the best snack," and on and on went the puns.

As for drinks, there is an enormous variety to choose from in T&T. Two brands of beer, Carib and Stag, vie for the title of most popular beer—even though both are owned by the same company. Stag was immortalized in song by Mighty Sparrow:

> The recession fighter,
> No beer is better...
> Fight the recession,
> Enjoy a refreshing—Stag!
> Stag is brewing something,
> Something about it!

Another popular drink is rum, which was originally known as "kill devil" in the West Indies. A "rum cork" is a boozer in Trini slang. T&T produce more than four million gallons of rum every year. The most popular brands are Old Oak and Vat 19. The traditional rum shop, where working-class men gathered after work, is disappearing in T&T, but British-style pubs have recently become popular. Numerous mixed drinks are made with rum and fruit juices, and we have included recipes for some of the favorites.

T&T has its share of unusual drinks. One is made with sea moss, a variety of kelp, which is cooked in a pressure cooker until it is gelatinous; it is then combined with lime, sugar, and milk. Another drink is a *mauby*, made from the bark of the carob tree (*Colubrina reclinata*)—the bark is also called *mauby*. This spicy drink is flavored with aniseed and is an acquired taste. So is a drink called "The Bomb," which is made with Guinness Stout, nutmeg, milk, and bitters. Speaking of bitters, Trinidad is the home of the Angostura Bitters Com-pany, so it is not surprising to find this herbal flavoring in many island drinks.

Another popular drink in Trindad is homemade wine, made from sugar cane, various tropical fruits such as mango, and unusual ingredients such as cashews. The common technique is to combine the wine ingredient with water and yeast and let it ferment for a couple of weeks. We have included a recipe for Pineapple Wine (page 44) as an example.

Doubles

Doubles are a very substantial snack indeed, with two of them making a meal. All of the doubles vendors in Port of Spain are certified by the Board of Health and wear health tags to prove it. Their stands undergo periodic spot inspections, and the regulations are very strict, so eating doubles on the street is not a health risk. Doubles are composed of two pieces of *bara* bread and a filling of *channa*, hot sauce, and *kucheela*. *Channa* is curried chick-peas, which are also known as garbanzo beans. Canned cooked garbanzos can be used, but the flavor will not be as good as that of the freshly cooked ones.

1 pound dried *channa* (chick-peas) *or*
   1 can (16 oz.) chick-peas, drained
6 to 8 cups water, plus 2 1/2 cups water
3 tablespoons West Indian Masala
   (page 34)
3 tablespoons canola or corn oil
5 cloves garlic, minced
1 onion, chopped
1 Congo pepper or Habanero, seeds and
   stem removed, minced
1 teaspoon ground cumin
Salt and freshly ground pepper, to taste
About 30 slices *bara* bread (your choice from
   Chapter 9)
Hot pepper sauce (your choice from
   Chapter 4), to taste
Mango Kucheela (page 37), to taste

Soak the *channa* in the 6 to 8 cups water overnight, or gently boil it with a little *masala* for about 3 hours.

Mix the *masala* with 1/2 cup of the water. Warm the oil in a large skillet over medium heat; add the garlic, onion, and *masala* mixed with water. Sauté for 2 to 3 minutes.

Drain the *channa*, add to skillet, and stir well. Add 1 1/2 cups of the water, Congo pepper, and cumin; cover and simmer, stirring occasionally, until the *channa* is very soft (about 1 hour). Add the remaining 1/2 cup of the water if the *channa* begins to dry out. Add salt and ground pepper, to taste.

To assemble doubles, spread the *channa* mixture on 1 piece of *bara* bread. Add the hot sauce and *kucheela,* to taste, then place another piece of *bara* bread on top to make a sandwich. Repeat with the remaining bread, *channa* mixture, hot sauce, and *kucheela*. Serve at once.

Yield: Makes at least 15 doubles.

Passion Fruit Cocktail

Passion fruit is just becoming available in the United States, mostly as canned juice. It is one of the finest-tasting tropical fruits, and when combined with rum, as in this old Creole recipe, it makes a superb cocktail for liming about.

4 ripe passion fruits *or* 1 cup passion
   fruit juice
4 ounces rum
2 teaspoons sugar
2 cups crushed ice
Angostura bitters
Freshly grated nutmeg

Squeeze the passion fruits and strain the juice. In a pitcher combine the juice with the rum, sugar, and ice; stir well. Pour the mixture into 4 glasses, add a dash of bitters and a sprinkle of nutmeg to each glass, and serve at once.

Yield: Makes 4 servings.

St. James Rum Punch

Rum punches are probably the most popular drinks in T&T. The rule-of-thumb formula for making West Indies rum punch calls for "one sour, two sweet, three strong, and four weak." Sour is lime or lemon juice, sweet is sugar syrup, strong is rum, and weak is water and ice. This version is weak on the weak.

1 cup sugar
1 cup water
1/2 cup freshly squeezed lime juice
1 1/2 cups rum
1 cup crushed ice
Angostura bitters
Freshly grated nutmeg

Make a sugar syrup by combining the sugar and the water and boiling the mixture, stirring constantly, for 5 minutes. Reduce the heat and simmer until all sugar has been dissolved. Remove from the heat and let cool.

Pour the cooled syrup into a pitcher. Add the lime juice, rum, and ice; stir thoroughly. Pour the mixture into 4 glasses; add a dash of bitters to each glass and sprinkle with grated nutmeg. Serve at once.

Yield: Makes 4 servings.

Las Piñas Coladas Verdaderas

These are the true piña coladas. Forget canned coconut cream—it's too sweet. Make this drink the way the Trinidadians do, and you'll never fix it any other way again.

1 cup white rum
1 1/2 cups coconut milk (page 36)
1 1/2 cups pineapple juice
1/2 cup diced fresh pineapple
1/2 cup whipping cream
6 cups crushed ice
4 wedges fresh pineapple, for garnish

Blend all of the ingredients except the pineapple wedges in a blender. Serve in 4 tall glasses over additional crushed ice, garnished with pineapple wedges.

Yield: Makes 4 servings.

Coconut Water Cocktails

Coconut water dwells in the center of immature coconuts and can easily be removed by cutting the top off the coconut with a machete. We have heard that coconut water is available bottled in some Caribbean markets, which is somewhat easier but more expensive. Coconut water is commonly used as a mixer in T&T, even for—believe it or not—Scotch. (It's much better than it sounds—take it from a pair of Scotch drinkers.) Reputedly, gin and coconut water is another popular T&T Sunday morning drink, as is Poncha Crema (page 43).

2 ounces Scotch, rum, or gin
5 or 6 ice cubes
Water from immature coconut(s)

Combine the liquor and ice cubes in a tall glass and fill with coconut water. Stir well and serve.

Yield: Makes 1 serving.

Congo Mary

Okay, okay, we admit it—we invented this drink. But with all the ingredients readily available, it seemed like a natural. Even tomatoes are plentiful in T&T.

5 ice cubes
1/2 ounce freshly squeezed lime juice
3 ounces tomato juice
1 teaspoon Johnny's Food Haven Pepper
    Sauce (page 33)
2 ounces white rum
Freshly ground black pepper, to taste
Chive or green onion stalk, for garnish

　　Combine all of the ingredients except the chive in a highball glass and stir well. Garnish with the chive and serve at once.

Yield: Makes 1 serving.

Poncha Crema

This Trinidadian eggnog is often called *ponche de creme*, but regardless of whether you're speaking Spanish or French, it still translates as cream punch. It is often served before breakfast on Sundays! There are many modern methods of making this drink, some of which use evaporated or condensed milk. But this is the old-fashioned recipe. Take care not to boil the mixture.

4 cups whole milk
6 eggs, beaten
1 cup sugar
3 cups white rum
1 teaspoon vanilla extract
4 to 5 drops Angostura bitters
Lime zest, for garnish
Freshly grated nutmeg, for garnish

　　In a medium saucepan over very low heat, warm the 4 cups milk. Cook for 7 minutes, stir regularly.
　　Add the eggs and sugar; stir and cook until the mixture thickens, taking care not to boil it or the eggs will curdle. Remove from the heat and let cool.
　　Add the rum, vanilla, and bitters; stir well. Refrigerate the mixture until ready to serve.
　　To serve, pour the mixture into 4 glasses, garnish with zest, and sprinkle with nutmeg.

Yield: Makes 4 servings.

Planter's Punch

The combination of sweet and sour is common in Trini drinks. This classic, featuring dark rum, is considered to be the most famous of all fruit punches. Any combination of fruit juices is allowed, but why not lime, orange, and pineapple?

4 ice cubes
3/4 ounce freshly squeezed lime juice
1/2 ounce grenadine
1 1/2 ounces freshly squeezed orange juice
1 1/2 ounces fresh pineapple juice
2 ounces dark rum
Dash Angostura bitters (optional)
Crushed ice
Lime slice, for garnish

In a shaker combine the ice cubes, lime juice, grenadine, orange juice, pineapple juice, rum, and bitters. Shake, then strain into a highball glass filled with crushed ice. Garnish with the lime slice and serve.

Yield: Makes 1 serving.

Maracas Bay Daiquiris

Cocktails at the beach? How decadent. Most folks just pop open a Carib. Of course, this concoction will have to be blended beforehand—unless you have one of those solar-powered blenders.

2 1/2 cups crushed ice
1 banana, peeled
1/2 cup freshly grated coconut
Juice of 1/2 lime, freshly squeezed
2 teaspoons superfine sugar
1/2 cup white rum

Combine all of the ingredients in a blender and blend at high speed for at least 30 seconds. Pour into champagne flutes, or paper cups if you must.

Yield: Makes 2 servings.

Pineapple Wine

A number of wines are made from T&T crops, including mangoes, sugar cane, rice, cashews, oranges, and passion fruit. We even found recipes for spinach wine and yam wine, but we weren't brave enough to try them. Following is the old-fashioned method of making fruit wine, and we have chosen pineapple. This concoction takes a month to prepare, so be patient.

2 pineapples, peeled and grated
8 cups water
1/2 pound raisins
2 pounds sugar
1 teaspoon active dry yeast
1/2 teaspoon ground mace (optional)

In a large pot combine the pineapple, water, raisins, and sugar. Bring to a boil, then reduce the heat and simmer for 10 minutes. Remove from the heat and let cool.

Transfer the mixture to a large glass container, add the yeast and mace, and cover loosely. Let stand for 2 weeks at room temperature.

Strain the mixture through cheesecloth, return it to the container, cover loosely, and let stand for another 2 weeks.

Restrain the mixture through a finer cloth, bottle it, and store in the refrigerator until ready to serve.

Yield: Makes about 8 cups.

The Mighty Quencher

Based on a number of old Trini recipes, this nonalcoholic combination of tropical juices will refresh the thirst of any jogger who has completed the loop around the Queen's Park Savannah.

1 large ripe mango, peeled, sliced, and puréed
1 cup pineapple juice
1 cup guava juice or passion fruit juice
1 cup freshly squeezed orange juice
1/4 cup freshly squeezed lime juice
1/4 cup grenadine
Dash Angostura bitters (optional)
Crushed ice
2 orange slices, for garnish

Combine all of the ingredients except the orange slices in a large pitcher and stir well. Serve in 2 highball glasses; garnish with the orange slices.

Yield: Makes 2 servings.

Ginger Beer

Although the flavor of ginger is readily available through commercial ginger ales, there's nothing quite as refreshing and intriguing as freshly made ginger beer. There are many variations of this recipe, including one with potatoes. One old Trini cookbook advised: "Addition of a small quantity of rum makes it a better keeper."

1 pound fresh ginger, peeled and grated
Juice and zest of 2 limes
1 tablespoon cream of tartar
4 quarts boiling water
2 teaspoons active dry yeast
3 cups sugar

In a large nonreactive bowl, combine the ginger, lime juice and zest, and cream of tartar. Pour the boiling water over top and allow to stand overnight.

Add the yeast and stir thoroughly; let stand for 10 minutes. Strain the mixture, then add the sugar and stir until it is dissolved. Store in sterilized bottles.

Yield: Makes about 4 quarts.

Hibiscus Sorrel Drink

Sorrel is the fleshy sepal of a species of hibiscus (*Hibiscus sabdariffa*), also known as *flor de jamaica* and *rosella*. We were quite surprised to find dried sorrel at our neighborhood supermarket in Albuquerque, so we assume it is available elsewhere.

2 cups dried sorrel
1 piece (1 in.) fresh ginger
1 piece (1 in.) dried orange zest
6 whole cloves
4 cups boiling water
1 cup sugar

Place the sorrel, ginger, orange zest, and cloves in a pitcher and pour the boiling water over top. Let stand for 24 hours.

Strain out the solids, then add the sugar to the liquid and stir until dissolved. Serve straight over ice or with rum as a cocktail.

Yield: Makes about 4 cups.

Duffy's Herbal Remedy

Do you suffer from indigestion or an upset stomach? If so, try the herbman's cure. Up in Paramin, Duffy Lamy gave us his recipe. The finest herbs in Trinidad are grown in Paramin, and it is only fitting that they have a multitude of uses.

1 teaspoon fresh basil *or*
  1/2 teaspoon dried basil
2 teaspoons fresh mint *or*
  1 teaspoon dried mint
1/2 teaspoon aniseed
1 cup boiling water

In a medium bowl combine the basil, mint, and aniseed. Pour the boiling water over top and allow to steep for 3 minutes. Strain the liquid into a cup and drink as needed.

Yield: Makes 1 serving.

Hot Avocado Dip with Plantain Chips

A nearly perfect appetizer, this is T&T's version of guacamole. Cooks should add the Congo pepper carefully and taste for heat, since this innocent-appearing dip can be incendiary to some palates.

Dip
2 ripe avocados, peeled and chopped
2 tomatoes, peeled and chopped
1 medium onion, minced
2 cloves garlic, minced
2 tablespoons minced fresh parsley *or*
  1 tablespoon minced cilantro
3 seasoning peppers or Yellow Wax Hots,
  seeds and stems removed, minced
1 tablespoon minced Congo pepper or
  Habanero

Chips
2 green plantains
Vegetable oil, for shallow frying

To make the dip, combine all of the ingredients in a bowl and mix well. Cover tightly with plastic wrap and chill until ready to use.

To make the chips, peel the plantains and slice as thin as possible. Heat the oil in the skillet over medium heat. Fry the slices in hot oil a dozen at a time. Drain on paper towels. Serve in a bowl with the dip.

Yield: Makes 4 servings of dip and dozens of chips.

Roasted Meat Kibby

George Raffoul, a member of Port of Spain's Lebanese community, says that this dish is served at his house with stuffed grape leaves or cabbage rolls, a tossed salad, and yogurt. We had our first taste of kibby at the Ali Baba restaurant in Maraval, a suburb of Port of Spain. Our kibby was served as an appetizer, but the dish is often served as an entrée.

1/2 cup bulgur (cracked wheat)
2 cups water
1/4 cup grated onion
Dash *each* salt and freshly ground pepper
1 1/2 pounds ground lamb
1 onion, finely chopped
Salt and freshly ground black pepper,
  to taste
1/4 cup pine nuts
2 teaspoons freshly squeezed lemon or
  lime juice
1/2 teaspoon ground cinnamon
Dash ground nutmeg
1/2 Congo pepper or Habanero, seeds and
  stem removed, finely chopped
Plain yogurt, for dipping

Soak the bulgur in the water for 30 minutes. Drain the bulgur well and squeeze out the excess water.

To make the coating, transfer the bulgur to a large bowl and add the grated onion, dash salt and pepper, and 1 pound of the lamb. Wet your hands and knead the mixture gently until it holds together. Set the coating aside while preparing the filling.

To make the filling, brown the remaining 1/2 pound lamb with the chopped onion, then drain thoroughly. Add the salt and pepper, to taste, pine nuts, lemon juice, cinnamon, nutmeg, and Congo pepper; mix well.

Wet your hands and scoop up enough coating to make a ball about 2 inches in diameter. With your finger make a hole in the center of the ball of coating; stuff the hole with some of the filling mixture. Close the hole by molding the coating mixture over it, then flatten the kibby into an oblong shape. The finished kibby should look like a flattened, elongated egg. Repeat until all mixtures are used up.

Place the finished kibbys on a greased baking sheet and bake in a 350 degree F oven until browned (20 to 30 minutes). Remove the kibbys from the baking sheet with a spatula and drain them on paper towels.

Serve the kibbys hot or at room temperature with a bowl of yogurt for dipping.

Yield: Makes 8 to 10 servings.

Chutney-Stuffed Eggs

This Trini variation of deviled eggs can be made with any of the chutneys in Chapter 4, or Mango Kucheela (page 37).

6 hard-cooked eggs, peeled
1/2 cup mayonnaise
3 tablespoons chutney (your choice from
  Chapter 4)

Cut the eggs in half and remove the yolks. Mash yolks thoroughly with a fork and combine with the mayonnaise and chutney until the mixture is well blended. Stuff the egg halves with mixture and serve.

Yield: Makes 12 egg halves.

Nancy's Blender Phulouri

Nancy Ramesar, an Irish woman married to a man of East Indian descent, has mastered the art of Trinidadian East Indian cooking and has discovered that the way to her man's heart includes curries and other spicy delights, such as this *phulouri*. She took Dave into her kitchen, tied an apron around him, and directed him to fry these little appetizers. Dave got bored frying tidy little round puffs, so much to her delight, he started making animal and vegetable shapes.

1 seasoning pepper or Yellow Wax Hot,
   seeds and stem removed, chopped
6 cloves garlic
1 pound split pea flour (see Note)
1 cup water
1 teaspoon salt
1/4 teaspoon ground cumin
1/4 teaspoon dried thyme
1 teaspoon West Indian Masala (page 34)
1 teaspoon baking powder
Soy or canola oil, for frying
Ramesar Mango Chutney, for dipping
   (page 37)

In a blender combine the seasoning pepper, garlic, split pea flour, water, salt, cumin, thyme, and *masala*. Blend on high speed until the mixture is thoroughly combined (about 1 1/2 minutes). Transfer the batter to a mixing bowl and whisk in the baking powder.

To determine if the batter is ready for frying, place a drop of it in a glass of cool water. If the batter floats, it is ready for frying. If it sinks, whip more air into the batter and test again.

Pour the oil into a large skillet over medium heat to a depth of 1 inch. Drop in the batter 1 tablespoon at a time and fry until golden brown (2 to 3 minutes). Drain on paper towels and keep warm in the oven until all the batter is fried. Serve with chutney for dipping.

Yield: Makes 6 to 10 servings.

Note: If split pea flour is not available at your local natural foods store, buy dried split peas and soak them overnight in water. Drain off the liquid and grind the peas in a blender, adding back some water if necessary. Then add the remaining ingredients and proceed. The peas can also be boiled in water until barely soft and then ground in the blender.

callaloo:
soups and salads

One of the signature dishes of T&T is callaloo, a thick dark green soup that's served everywhere on the two islands. It is thought to be of African origin, and variations of it appear all over the Caribbean. Although it changes slightly from island to island, two ingredients are standard: okra and callaloo leaves, also known as taro, *dasheen*, or *tannia*. The plant is an aroid, related to the inedible philodendron. The meat that is added to callaloo can be anything from pig's tails to crab meat; the spices range from Congo peppers to cloves. The soup is often served in T&T homes on Sundays and special occasions.

Trinis seem to eat more soups than salads, which is why the soups outnumber the salads in this chapter. Most of the soups feature Congo peppers, which are left whole and then removed before serving. They give the soup a bite without overwhelming it, but care should be taken not to let the pepper burst or the pungency might be overpowering.

After callaloo, the two other most popular soups are *cowheel* and *sancoche*. *Cowheel* is a thick soup flavored with onions; *sancoche* is a kind of melting pot soup to which any number of vegetables are added. Pepperpot, which is served on many other islands, is also a favorite. Two unusual soups are Fish Tea, which is also served as a drink, and Chip-Chip Chowder, which is the Trini version of clam chowder.

As might be expected, fruits and avocados make their appearance in T&T salads. As a rule, salads are somewhat ordinary, but we managed to find some interesting ones. We have also included a recipe for *baba ganoush*, a Lebanese salad that is popular not only in Lebanese homes but also in restaurants.

Callaloo

This remarkable dark green soup is often called the national dish of T&T. As prepared by chefs Keith Toby and Irvine Jackson of the Cafe Savannah, it features callaloo (taro leaves or *dasheen*), but spinach is an excellent substitute.

3 bunches callaloo or fresh spinach, washed,
   tough ribs removed, coarsely chopped
4 cups coconut milk (page 36)
2 cups whole milk
2 cloves garlic, minced
2 medium onions, chopped
1 bunch green onions, chopped
1/4 pound pumpkin or hubbard squash,
   peeled and coarsely chopped
1/2 cup butter or margarine
Salt and freshly ground pepper, to taste

In a stockpot or soup pot, combine all of the ingredients and boil for 4 minutes. Reduce the heat and simmer for 40 minutes. If too thick, add more coconut milk.

Remove from the heat and let cool, then purée in a blender in small batches. Reheat the soup and serve at once.

Yield: Makes 8 to 10 servings.

Crab Meat Callaloo

Some people in T&T hold the belief that the way for a woman to catch a husband is to feed him her best callaloo. We ate this soup at every opportunity in order to sample its multiple variations, and even dined on it during our final dinner in T&T; it was the only thing that cheered us up as we thought about leaving the country. This variation features crab meat, a common and tasty addition.

2 tablespoons butter
1 medium onion, diced
1/2 cup chopped celery
1 clove garlic, minced
4 cups chicken stock
1 cup coconut milk (page 36)
1/2 pound smoked ham, diced, *or*
   1 small ham hock
2 1/2 cups washed, coarsely chopped,
   firmly packed callaloo (*dasheen*) or
   spinach leaves
1 cup sliced okra
1 teaspoon dried thyme
1/4 teaspoon freshly ground black pepper
1 Congo pepper or Habanero, seeds and
   stem removed, minced
1 pound cooked crab meat, chopped
1 tablespoon butter (optional)
Salt, to taste

    In a large saucepan over medium heat, melt the 2 tablespoons butter. Add the onion, celery, and garlic; sauté for 2 to 3 minutes. Add the stock, coconut milk, and ham and bring to a boil. Add the callaloo, okra, thyme, ground pepper, and Congo pepper. Cover the pot, reduce the heat to low, and simmer, stirring occasionally, until the callaloo is thoroughly cooked (about 50 minutes).

    Whisk the soup until very smooth, or purée it in small batches in a blender. Add the crab meat and heat thoroughly. Add the 1 tablespoon butter (if desired), swizzled over the top, and taste for salt. Serve hot.

Yield: Makes 8 to 10 servings.

Fish Tea

Also called fish broth and Creole bouillabaisse in T&T, this interesting concoction is either served in bowls as a soup or is drunk from glasses. It can also be used as a stock for other fish dishes. It is usually served with the bread called Hops (page 84) and boiled green "figs"—tiny but tasty bananas.

3 pounds fish, including heads
1 cup plus 2 tablespoons freshly squeezed
   lime juice
4 cups water
1 large onion, chopped
1 carrot, sliced
1 teaspoon minced fresh thyme
1 teaspoon minced fresh parsley
1 tablespoon minced chives or
   green onions
1/2 Congo pepper or Habanero, seeds and
   stems removed, left whole
1 teaspoon salt
1 bay leaf
1/2 cup butter
2 tablespoons dry sherry

    Clean and wash the fish. Marinate in 1 cup of the lime juice for at least 1 hour.

    Bring the water to a boil and add the onion, carrot, thyme, parsley, chives, Congo pepper, salt, bay leaf, and the 2 tablespoons lime juice. Boil for 5 minutes, then add the marinated fish. Boil for 20 minutes.

    Remove the fish from the pot. Add the butter and sherry and stir well. Strain the "tea" and serve warm.

Yield: Makes four 1-cup servings.

Pepperpot

Food historians believe that this dish originated in South America and was spread throughout the West Indies by the Arawaks. The key ingredient is *cassareep*, which is the boiled-down juice of raw cassava. It is available bottled in West Indian markets (and some Asian markets), or by mail order. Legend holds that in the early days, a pepperpot was always in the kitchen, and more meat was added to it each day, keeping the pot going for years.

1 pound cow's tail, cut into joints
1 cow's foot (ankle), quartered, or 2 beef
    marrow bones, washed
1 pound beef, cut into 1-inch cubes
1 pound pork, cut into 1-inch cubes
2 onions, chopped
2 Congo peppers or Habaneros, tied in a
    cheesecloth bag
1/2 cup *cassareep*
Salt and freshly ground pepper, to taste

Place the meats in a stew pot. Add the onions, Congo peppers, and *cassareep*. Add water to cover; bring to a boil, then reduce the heat and simmer until the meats are tender and nearly falling apart (about 2 hours). Add salt and ground pepper, to taste, and serve hot.

Yield: Makes 8 servings.

Zaboca Cream Soup

T&T soups are commonly based on local fruits and vegetables such as these avocados, breadfruit, and pumpkins. The addition of the Congo pepper is optional.

2 large, ripe avocados, cubed
1/2 teaspoon ground white pepper
1 cup whipping cream
4 cups chicken stock, preferably homemade
2 teaspoons Nancy's Seasoning Paste (page 36)
    or any seasoning mixture in Chapter 4
1 Congo pepper or Habanero, left whole
    (optional)
1/3 cup dry sherry
Salt, to taste
Extremely thin avocado slices, for garnish

In a blender or food processor, purée the avocados, ground pepper, and cream.

Heat the stock in a large saucepan until just boiling; slowly stir in the avocado purée and seasoning paste. Reduce the heat, add the Congo pepper, and simmer until slightly thickened (15 to 20 minutes), stirring occasionally.

Add the sherry. Remove the Congo pepper, stir, adjust for salt, and remove from the heat. Pour into bowls, garnish with avocado slices, and serve.

Yield: Makes 4 to 6 servings.

Cowheel Soup

This very traditional T&T soup is served at Johnny's Food Haven, where it is prepared fresh each day. Beef ankle bones, a substitute for *cowheel*, are available at most specialty butcher shops. Cubed hubbard, acorn, or butternut squash can be added along with the celery and green onions. Dumplings or 1/2 cup raw rice can be added during the last 15 to 20 minutes of cooking.

1 cowheel *or* 2 pounds beef ankle bones,
  cut into 1 1/2-inch sections, *or* 2 pounds
  soup bones, including 1 marrow bone
1/2 cup chopped celery
2 green onions, chopped
3 cloves garlic, chopped
3/4 cup sliced carrots
1 teaspoon dried thyme
1 small Congo pepper or Habanero, left whole
Salt, to taste
1 teaspoon freshly squeezed lemon juice
  (optional)

Wash and clean the cowheel. Place in a large pot and cover with water. Bring to a boil, then reduce the heat and simmer for 1 hour, uncovered, adding more water if necessary and skimming off any foam that rises to the top.

Add the celery, onions, garlic, carrots, thyme, Congo pepper, and salt. Cook, covered, for 1 1/2 hours, adding more water if necessary.

Remove and discard the Congo pepper. Remove the bones from the soup and cut off any meat, returning the meat to soup. Add lemon juice, if desired, and reheat the soup. Serve hot.

Yield: Makes 6 servings.

Chip-Chip Chowder

The flavor of these small mollusks is nearly identical to that of littleneck clams, so they would be the best substitute. The principal differences between this tropical chowder and the New England or Manhattan versions served in the States is the addition of a Congo pepper and the absence of cream or tomatoes.

48 clams
4 cups water
Chicken stock, as needed
1 pound *tannias* or potatoes, peeled and diced
1 large onion, chopped
2 green onions (including green tops), chopped
1 teaspoon minced fresh thyme
1 Congo pepper or Habanero, left whole
2 tablespoons butter
1 tablespoon freshly squeezed lime juice
Shadow Bennie (*culantro*), cilantro, or
  minced parsley, for garnish

Wash the clams and place them in a large pot. Add the water and cook until the clam shells open. Discard any unopened clams.

Remove the clam meat and discard the necks. Set aside the meat. Strain broth through muslin, measure the liquid, and combine with enough chicken stock to make 6 cups liquid. Return the liquid to the pot.

Add the *tannias*, onion, green onions, thyme, and Congo pepper; cook over medium heat until the *tannias* are tender (about 30 minutes).

Remove the Congo pepper. Strain the broth again and reserve; purée the *tannia* mixture in a blender. Return the purée to pot with the broth; add the reserved clams, butter, and lime juice and simmer until thickened (5 to 10 minutes). Garnish with Shadow Bennie and serve.

Yield: Makes 6 servings.

Chicken Soup Arima

This flavorful soup shows the Chinese influence on a Creole dish. The vegetables should be fairly crunchy. Serve it with wontons or egg rolls.

2 tablespoons olive oil
2 cups diced raw chicken meat
2 cups boiling water
1/4 cup chopped onion
1/2 cup chopped cucumber
1 cup bamboo shoots
1/2 cup diced carrot
1 cup water chestnuts
1/2 cup chopped mushrooms
2 tablespoons All-Purpose Seasoning Mixture
   (page 35)
Salt, to taste
1/2 cup toasted slivered almonds

   Heat the oil in a large saucepan over medium heat. Add the chicken and sauté for about 15 minutes, stirring often. Add the water, onion, cucumber, bamboo shoots, carrot, water chestnuts, mushrooms, seasoning mixture, and salt. Bring to a boil, then reduce the heat and simmer, uncovered, for about 10 minutes. Garnish with the almonds and serve hot.

Yield: Makes 4 servings.

T&T Split Pea Soup

Here is your basic T&T comfort soup, a familiar friend that has many variations in the islands. Some recipes call for the addition of pumpkin, sweet potatoes, corn, and taro root, but we have stuck with a more basic—though hot and spicy—approach.

1 cup dried split peas
8 cups water
1 onion, chopped
2 cloves garlic, chopped
1 tablespoon All-Purpose Seasoning Mixture
   (page 35)
1 ham bone
2 teaspoons minced fresh thyme
1 Congo pepper or Habanero, left whole

   Soak the peas in 4 cups of the water for several hours. Drain and rinse the peas and place them in a large pot. Add the remaining 4 cups water, onion, garlic, seasoning mixture, ham bone, thyme, and Congo pepper. Bring to a boil, then reduce the heat and simmer until the peas are soft and thick (about 2 hours).
   Cut the meat off the bone and return it to the soup. Stir well and reheat. Remove the ham bone and Congo pepper before serving.

Yield: Makes 4 servings.

Sancoche

Depending on the cook, this versatile stew can contain up to nine starchy ingredients, including yams, *tannia*, taro, cassava, bananas, potatoes, pumpkin, and plantains. But since many of these ingredients are both hard to find and are similar in flavor, we have adjusted the recipe somewhat. The name derives from South American stews called *sancochos*; other names for it include plantation stew. Noted Creole chef Jean de Boissiere said: "This is the all-filling, midday meal of rich and poor alike on the plantations of Trinidad." It is particularly popular for Saturday lunch in T&T.

3 tablespoons vegetable oil
1/2 pound corned beef, cut into 1-inch cubes
1 pound beef, cut into 1-inch cubes
2 large onions, chopped
8 cups beef stock
1 tablespoon Paramin Herb Seasoning (page 36)
1 cup yellow split peas or black-eyed peas
1 cup coconut cream (page 36)
1 pound sweet potatoes or yams, peeled
  and cut into 1-inch cubes
2 green plantains, peeled and thickly sliced
2 pounds potatoes, peeled and cut into
  1-inch cubes
1 Congo pepper or Habanero, left whole
Salt and freshly ground pepper, to taste
Hops (page 84), for accompaniment

In a large skillet over medium heat, warm the oil. Sauté the corned beef and other beef cubes until slightly browned, then add the onions and sauté for 5 minutes, stirring occasionally. Add the stock, herb seasoning, and split peas; reduce the heat, cover, and simmer for 1 hour.

Add all of the remaining ingredients and simmer, covered, until the potatoes are tender (about 30 minutes), adding more water if necessary.

Remove the Congo pepper, add salt and pepper to taste, and serve hot with Hops.

Yield: Makes 6 to 8 servings.

Black-eyed Pea and Coconut Soup

Black-eyed peas do not appear in recipes as often as split peas, but they are popular in T&T. Some versions of this soup call for the addition of sweet potatoes, pumpkin, and taro root, but we prefer to keep this dish a soup rather than a stew. You may want to purée the soup in a blender before adding the ham and Congo pepper. You can also add 1/4 cup dry sherry or rum to the soup just before serving.

1 cup black-eyed peas
12 cups water
2 onions
1 ham bone
1 tablespoon Paramin Herb Seasoning (page 36)
1 tablespoon vegetable oil
2 tomatoes, peeled and chopped
2 1/2 cups coconut milk (page 36)
1 Congo pepper or Habanero, left whole

Soak the peas in 4 cups of the water overnight. Drain, rinse, and place in a large pot with the remaining 8 cups water. Chop one of the onions and add it to the pan. Add the ham bone and herb seasoning; bring to a boil and boil rapidly for 15 minutes, skimming off any foam that might rise. Reduce the heat and simmer until the peas are done (about 45 minutes).

Remove the ham bone; trim off the remaining meat and reserve.

In a small skillet over medium heat, warm the oil. Chop the remaining onion and add it and the tomatoes to the skillet; sauté for about 3 minutes. Add this and the coconut milk to the soup. Bring to a boil, then reduce the heat, add the reserved ham and Congo pepper, and cook until the soup thickens (about 20 minutes). Remove the Congo pepper before serving.

Yield: Makes 6 servings.

Cream of Pumpkin Soup with Congo Pepper

Pumpkin is very popular in T&T and appears in recipes ranging from soups to desserts. Hubbard squash is an adequate substitute in the United States.

1 pound hubbard squash, peeled and chopped
1 onion, chopped
3 cups chicken stock
1 Congo pepper or Habanero, left whole
1/2 cup whipping cream
1/4 teaspoon ground cinnamon
Salt and freshly ground pepper, to taste
Cilantro leaves, for garnish

In a large saucepan combine the squash, onion, stock, and Congo pepper. Bring to a boil, then reduce the heat to low and simmer until the squash is tender (20 to 30 minutes). Remove from the heat, remove the Congo pepper, and purée the mixture in a blender.

Return the mixture to the pan; add the cream and cinnamon and cook over low heat until thickened. Add salt and pepper, to taste. Garnish with the cilantro and serve.

Yield: Makes 4 servings.

Nancy's Dhal

In this version of *dhal*, as taught to us by Nancy Ramesar, the finished dish can be used as a soup or as a sauce over rice or other vegetarian or meat dishes.

1 pound yellow split peas, washed and cleaned
1 tablespoon Nancy's Seasoning Paste (page 36)
1 tablespoon Trinidadian Curry Paste (page 35)
1 1/2 teaspoons salt
2 teaspoons cumin seeds
2 tablespoons vegetable oil
4 cloves garlic, crushed
1 onion, chopped
1 seasoning pepper or Yellow Wax Hot,
    seeds and stem removed, chopped

Place the split peas in a heavy casserole dish, cover with water, and bring to a boil. Reduce the heat and simmer for 1 to 1 1/2 hours.

Transfer the mixture to a blender or food processor and purée until slightly soupy. Return the purée to the casserole dish, add the pastes and salt, and simmer.

Meanwhile, roast the cumin seeds in a dry skillet over medium heat until they turn dark (about 2 minutes). Shake the skillet and take care that the seeds do not burn. Add to the puréed mixture.

In a small skillet over medium heat, heat the oil. Add the garlic, onion, and seasoning pepper; sauté, stirring occasionally, until the mixture turns very dark brown—almost black. Add to the puréed mixture and stir until heated through. Serve in a tureen as a sauce or in bowls as a soup.

Yield: Makes 4 soup servings or 6 sauce servings.

Baba Ganoush

Eggplants are called *melongenes* in Trinidad, and they are eaten in one form or another by every ethnic group. George Raffoul, a clothing manufacturer, gave us this quick and versatile recipe for Lebanese eggplant salad. This substantial salad is best served at room temperature.

1 medium to large eggplant
1 cup minced cooked lamb
1 medium onion, finely chopped
4 cloves garlic, smashed and finely chopped
1/3 cup chopped fresh parsley
2 1/2 tablespoons freshly squeezed lime juice
2 tomatoes, diced (optional)
4 lettuce leaves, for serving
Toasted pita bread, for accompaniment

Slit the eggplant with a knife in 3 or 4 places; bake in a 350 degree F oven until soft (about 1 hour). Let cool, then peel and finely dice.

In a large bowl combine the diced eggplant, lamb, onion, garlic, parsley, lime juice, and tomatoes (if desired); mix well. Allow the mixture to stand for 30 minutes for the flavors to blend. Serve on individual lettuce leaves with toasted pita bread.

Yield: Makes 4 servings.

Creole Fruit Salad

This salad, which celebrates the abundance of fruit in T&T, is not only simple to make, it's easily changed depending upon which fruits are in season. Simply add or subtract fruits from this combination.

2 oranges, peeled and segmented,
   segments cut in half
2 mangoes, peeled and diced
1 small papaya, peeled, seeded, and diced
2 bananas, peeled and sliced
1/2 pineapple, peeled and diced
2 tablespoons sugar
Lettuce leaves, for serving
1 cup fresh grated coconut or dried, unsweetened
   shredded coconut

In a large bowl combine the fruits; add the sugar and mix well. To serve, place lettuce leaves on individual plates, spoon the fruit on top, and sprinkle with grated coconut.

Yield: Makes 6 servings.

Mixed Seafood Salad

Ideally, the best-tasting seafood is cooked when fresh. But we won't tell if cooks wish to substitute frozen or canned seafood if fresh is not available.

Salad
1 cup cooked shrimp
1 cup cooked lobster meat
1 cup cooked crab meat
1 cup sliced celery
1/2 cup chopped onion
1/4 cup minced fresh parsley *or* 1/8 cup
   minced cilantro
1 cup minced cucumber
1/2 cup sliced green olives (optional)
Lettuce leaves or spinach leaves,
   for serving
Minced tops of green onions, for garnish

Dressing
1 cup plain yogurt
1/2 teaspoon prepared mustard
1/2 teaspoon minced garlic
2 tablespoons freshly squeezed lime juice
1/2 teaspoon hot sauce (your choice from
   Chapter 4, or any commercial
   Habanero sauce)
Salt, to taste

To make the salad, in a large bowl combine the shrimp, lobster, crab, celery, onion, parsley, cucumber, and olives (if used); mix well.

To make the dressing, combine all of the ingredients and mix well. Pour over the salad and toss. (Refrigerate any unused dressing.)

To serve, arrange the salad on lettuce leaves and garnish with green onions.

Yield: Makes 4 salad servings and 1 cup dressing.

Lobster-Stuffed Zabocas

Zabocas are avocados, one of the most important of all the island fruits; they are native to Central America. In this recipe, feel free to substitute any cooked seafood for the lobster. Be sure to peel the avocados right before using so they don't turn brown.

1 to 1 1/2 cups cooked lobster meat
   (depending on the size of the avocados)
1 teaspoon freshly squeezed lime juice
1 tablespoon All-Purpose Seasoning
   Mixture (page 35)
2 ripe avocados, peeled, pits removed,
   and halved
Lettuce leaves, for serving

In a large bowl combine the lobster meat, lime juice, and seasoning mixture; stir thoroughly. Fill the avocado halves with the mixture and serve on lettuce leaves.

Yield: Makes 4 servings.

Island Coleslaw

This salad features some of the produce we found during our visit to the Central Market in Port of Spain. The Trinis love cabbage and often combine it with fruits.

1 small cabbage, shredded (about 4 1/2 to
   5 cups)
1/2 cup crushed fresh pineapple
1/2 cup finely sliced orange sections
1/2 cup diced mangoes
1 cup plain yogurt
Dasheen or spinach leaves, for serving

In a large bowl combine the cabbage, pineapple, orange sections, mangoes, and yogurt; mix well. Serve on a bed of *dasheen*.

Yield: Makes 6 servings.

Pelau:
Meat and
chicken dishes

We never had a chance to try the local delicacies such as agouti, *tatoo* (armadillo), *quenk* (peccary), or *manicou* (opossum), but we ate just about every other meat-bearing animal or bird on the islands. The Trinis consumed fifty-nine pounds of meat per person in 1970, mostly beef and pork, but this figure is limited by the meat prohibitions of Hindus and Muslims. The Hindus do not eat beef and Muslims abstain from pork. The result is that everyone eats chicken. In 1975 Trinis were the second-heaviest poultry consumers in the world, averaging nearly twenty-five pounds per person per year. The popularity of chicken is reflected in Lord Christo's 1968 calypso, "Chicken Chest," which tells the story of a woman who steals a box of frozen chicken breasts from the Hi-Lo grocery:

> When Constable take back the chicken,
> I watch this woman and start to grin.
> She caught a cramp and fall down twice.
> Her tummy was so cold as a block of ice.

Much of the chicken is consumed at fast food locations such as Kentucky Fried Chicken and the Royal Castles. See Chapter 3 for the story of the "chicken wars." Many of the meat dishes in this chapter are classically Creole, such as *pelau*, black pudding, trotter souse, *pastelles*, and garlic pork, an import from Guyana. The recipes have changed very little in the hundreds of years they've been prepared on the islands.

One of the most popular ways to consume meat or chicken is with *roti*, a West Indian creation with an East Indian influence, consisting of curried meat, fowl, fish, or vegetables wrapped in griddle-baked flat bread (page 82). *Roti* shops are everywhere in T&T, and *roti* is particularly popular for lunch.

We searched our collection of calypso music for references to meat and poultry dishes, and came up with the following lines from Mighty Sparrow, who jokingly sang about "cannibalism" in his risque calypso "Congo Man."

> Two white women traveling through Africa,
> Find themselves in the hands of a cannibal head
>   hunter.
> He cook one up and he eat one raw,
> They taste so good, he wanted more.
> I envy the Congo Man,
> Ah wish ah coulda go and shake he hand.
> He eat until his stomach upset,
> And I, ah never eat ah white meat yet!

Pelau

The process of caramelizing meat is an African practice that became part of the Creole culinary tradition. The process gives the *pelau* its dark brown color—a sure sign of goodness. The brown layer that forms on the bottom of the pot is called "bun-bun"; for some people, it's their favorite part of the meal. This recipe comes from Johnny's Food Haven; the dish is served with Mango Kucheela (page 37).

3 tablespoons vegetable oil
3/4 cup sugar (granulated or brown)
1 chicken (2 1/2 to 3 lb.), cut up, or goat meat
    or beef (see Note)
1 onion, chopped
1 clove garlic, minced
1 1/2 cups pigeon peas or black-eyed peas,
    soaked overnight
2 cups rice (not instant)
3 cups water
1 cup coconut milk (page 36)
2 cups cubed hubbard squash
2 carrots, chopped
1/4 cup chopped fresh parsley
1 teaspoon dried thyme
1 bunch green onions, including green tops,
    chopped
1/4 cup catsup
3 tablespoons butter

In a heavy pot or skillet over high heat, heat the oil. Add the sugar and let it caramelize until almost burned, stirring constantly. Add the chicken and stir until all pieces are coated with the sugar. Reduce the heat to medium, add the onion and garlic, and cook, stirring constantly, for 1 minute. Drain the peas and add to the pot along with the rice, the water, and the coconut milk. Reduce the heat to low and simmer, covered, for 30 minutes. Add all of the remaining ingredients and stir until well mixed. Cover and cook until the vegetables are tender (20 to 30 minutes). The *pelau* should be moist at the end of the cooking time. Serve hot.

Yield: Makes 4 to 6 servings.

Note: If meat other than chicken is used (such as cubed goat meat or beef), parboil the meat for 45 minutes, then proceed as above.

Stewed Oxtail

This cut of meat, though bony, is quite tasty and comes from a cow rather than an ox. Many restaurants serve this dish with dumplings, green vegetables, and lentils. It's also good with yams or potatoes that are drizzled with butter and sprinkled with chopped parsely. Another option is to serve it with Sauteed Cassava (page 90).

2 tablespoons vegetable oil
3 pounds oxtails (beef tails), washed, dried, and cut into 2-inch sections
2 onions, coarsely chopped
3 cloves garlic, finely chopped
1 teaspoon dried thyme
3 carrots, cut into 1-inch pieces
2 tablespoons hot sauce (your choice from Chapter 4, or use bottled Habanero sauce) or 1/2 Congo pepper or Habanero, seeds and stems removed, minced
1/2 teaspoon freshly ground black pepper
3 cups beef stock
3 cups water, or more as needed
1 cup split peas or beans
Salt, to taste
1 tablespoon rum or 2 tablespoons dry sherry (optional)

In a large pot over medium heat, heat the oil. Add the oxtails and cook until browned. Add the onions and garlic and sauté for 1 minute. Add the thyme, carrots, hot sauce, and ground pepper; sauté for 2 minutes. Add the stock and the water and bring to a boil. Add the split peas; reduce the heat, cover, and simmer for 2 1/2 hours, stirring occasionally and checking the water level to avoid burning. Add more water if necessary.

The meat should be falling off the bones; if it isn't, simmer for another 30 minutes. Just before serving, skim any fat off the top and add salt and rum, if desired. The stew, if thin, can be served in a bowl; otherwise, serve it on a plate.

Yield: Makes 6 to 8 servings.

Variation
The Creole version of this dish calls for caramelizing the sugar with vegetable oil until it is almost burned, then adding the oxtails and proceeding as above.

Trotter Souse

This dish is popular in Barbados as well as T&T, and it's often served for Sunday breakfast with black pudding (page 62), which is really a sausage. For people who are squeamish about eating pig's feet (trotters), pork stew meat may be substituted. Note that the meat must marinate for at least six hours or preferably overnight.

4 pounds pig's feet, cut into small pieces
4 cloves garlic, minced
1 onion, thinly sliced
1 Congo pepper or Habanero, seeds and stem removed, finely chopped
1 1/2 cups freshly squeezed lime juice
3 to 4 cups water
1 teaspoon salt
2 cucumbers, peeled and chopped
1/2 teaspoon freshly ground black pepper
Watercress, for garnish

Place the cut-up trotters in a large pot, cover with salted water, and cook over medium heat until meat is tender (about 2 hours). Remove the meat from the water, rinse in cold water, and drain.

In a large bowl combine the cooked meat, garlic, onion, Congo pepper, lime juice, the water, salt, cucumbers, and ground pepper. Marinate for at least 6 hours or preferably overnight. Serve cold in bowls like a stew, garnished with the watercress.

Yield: Makes 8 servings.

Trinidad Black Pudding

Often served as an accompaniment to trotter souse (page 61), black pudding is actually a type of sausage. It was traditionally made with pig's blood, but nowadays liver is substituted.

1 pound liver, minced
2 tablespoons lemon juice
Salt and freshly ground pepper, to taste
1 pound sweet potatoes, peeled and grated
2 cups beef stock
1/2 pound pork fat, minced
1 cup water
2 tablespoons butter
1/4 teaspoon ground allspice
2 green onions, minced
2 tablespoons minced fresh thyme
2 large onions, minced
1 clove garlic, minced
3 seasoning peppers or Yellow Wax Hots,
   seeds and stems removed, minced
1/2 Congo pepper or Habanero, seeds and
   stem removed, minced
1 tablespoon catsup
1 tablespooon Worcestershire sauce
1/4 cup dried bread crumbs

In a large bowl combine the liver, lemon juice, salt, ground pepper, sweet potatoes, and stock; let stand for 20 minutes. Meanwhile, cook the pork fat in the water until all the water has evaporated, then remove from the heat and set aside.

In a large skillet over medium heat, melt the butter; add the allspice, green onions, thyme, onions, garlic, seasoning peppers, and Congo pepper. Sauté for 10 minutes. Add the catsup and Worcestershire sauce and mix well.

In a large bowl combine the liver mixture, reserved pork fat, sautéed seasonings, and bread crumbs; blend well. The mixture should be very soft. Fashion the mixture into a cylindrical shape and place on a greased sheet of aluminum foil. Wrap the mixture tightly in foil and place in a pan of boiling water. Simmer for 1 hour over low heat. Drain and let cool slightly before serving.

Yield: Makes 6 servings.

Herb-Marinated Roast Venison

This Creole dish, in the style of Jean de Boissiere, originated as the preferred method of roasting game, particularly entire legs of deer. Beef and pork roasts may also be prepared in this manner; however, you must increase the cooking time for pork. Serve this dish with potatoes and Island Coleslaw (page 58). Onions and green onions can be roasted in the same pan with the meat. Note that roast must stand for at least four hours or preferably overnight to absorb flavors from the seasoning mix. Some cooks prefer to cover the roast with aluminum foil while it cooks.

1 venison roast (about 4 lb.)
1 cup Paramin Herb Seasoning (page 36)
4 tablespoons butter, melted
5 slices bacon
6 to 8 potatoes, scrubbed
1/4 cup flour mixed with 1 cup water
Salt, to taste
1/4 cup brandy

Score the roast with cuts 1 inch deep and 1 inch apart. Fill the cuts with herb seasoning and let stand, covered, for at least 4 hours or preferably overnight in the refrigerator.

Spread the butter over the roast, and arrange the bacon slices perpendicular to the scores. Place the meat in a roasting pan, surround with the potatoes, and cook, uncovered, in a 350 degree F oven until the meat is medium-rare (20 minutes per pound, or about 1 hour and 20 minutes for a 4-pound roast). Baste occasionally with the pan drippings.

Remove the roast and potatoes from the pan and keep warm. To make the gravy, skim the excess fat off the pan drippings, and scrape the drippings from the bottom of the pan. Add the flour mixture and heat, stirring, until the gravy thickens. Taste and adjust for salt; add the brandy, stir, and remove from the heat.

To serve, slice the roast and serve it with the potatoes. Pour gravy over each serving.

Yield: Makes 6 to 8 servings.

Old-Style Holiday Pastelles

Tamales are traditionally served during the Christmas holidays all over the New World, and T&T is no exception. These *pastelles* (filled pastries), with their banana leaf wrap, are clearly more influenced by the Central American style than by the Mexican. This version features the old way of using corn, rather than making a dough from cornmeal.

1/3 cup vegetable oil
1 pound beef steak, minced or ground
1 pound lean pork, minced or ground
1 small onion, minced
1 small bunch green onions, including
 green tops, minced
1 clove garlic, minced
3 medium tomatoes, diced
1 tablespoon distilled white vinegar
1/4 cup raisins, minced (optional)
2 tablespoons capers (optional)
10 green olives, minced (optional)
Salt and freshly ground black pepper,
 to taste
12 pieces banana leaf, each 7 inches
 square, for wrapping
Vegetable oil, for coating leaves
3 cups grated fresh corn, excess juice
 squeezed out

In a large pot over medium heat, heat the 1/3 cup oil. Add the meat and cook until browned. Add the onion, green onions, garlic, tomatoes, vinegar, optional ingredients (if desired), and salt and ground pepper; cook for 15 minutes. The mixture should be fairly dry.

Coat the inside of the banana leaves with oil. Divide the corn among the leaves and spread it about 5 inches square and 1/4 inch thick on each leaf. Divide the meat mixture among the leaves (about 2 tablespoons per leaf) and spread it over the corn layer. Fold up the leaves into envelope-like packages and secure with cotton string.

Cook the *pastelles* for 1 hour, either in a large pot of boiling water or by steaming them on a rack over boiling water.

Yield: Makes 12 *pastelles*.

Solimar Pasta Bowl

Solimar Restaurant chef Joe Brown has substituted ripe plantains for pasta in this unusual dish. The melding of tastes and textures gives this creation an exotic twist. The casserole can be assembled an hour or two before serving, then the egg and cheese mixture can be added and the casserole baked.

1/4 cup soy oil or canola oil
2 pounds beef, minced (not ground)
4 seasoning peppers or Yellow Wax Hots,
 seeds and stems removed, chopped
2 cloves garlic, crushed
1 tablespoon chopped Shadow Bennie
 (*culantro*) or cilantro
1 large onion, chopped
1 large tomato, diced
1/4 cup tomato paste
1/4 cup beef or chicken stock
1/2 pound *bodi* beans or fresh green beans,
 cut into 2-inch lengths
5 large ripe plantains
4 eggs
1/2 cup grated Cheddar cheese

In a large skillet over medium heat, heat the oil; add the meat and sauté for 1 minute. Add the peppers, garlic, Shadow Bennie, and onion; sauté until the meat starts to brown. Add the tomato, tomato paste, and stock and cook for 10 minutes.

Blanch the beans for 2 minutes. Slice the plantains lengthwise into thin strips. Arrange the strips in a single layer on the bottom of a greased 9- by 13-inch baking dish. Alternate layers of the meat mixture, beans, and plantains, ending with plantains.

Beat the eggs and add the cheese. Pour over the mixture in the casserole dish and bake in a 350 degree F oven until golden brown (30 to 40 minutes).

Yield: Makes 6 to 8 servings.

Garlic Pork

This very traditional Portuguese island dish probably originated in Guyana. Our main culinary guide in Trinidad, Michael Coelho, told us that years ago his father would slaughter a pig, cut it up, and marinate it in a huge quantity of garlic, malt vinegar, and fresh thyme. After a week, the meat was cooked in a large pot, creating its own garlic oil. Although Trinis now forego the slaughtering and buy their pork at the Hi-Lo Supermarkets, the flavor is still strong and memorable! Note that the pork needs to marinate for at least two days or preferably a week.

1/4 pound garlic cloves
2 tablespoons fresh thyme *or* 4 tablespoons
   dried thyme
2 onions, chopped
1 Congo pepper or Habanero, seeds and
   stem removed, chopped
2 teaspoons salt
Juice of 1 lime
2 cups distilled white vinegar
4 pounds boneless pork leg or shoulder,
   cut into 1-inch cubes
Vegetable oil, for frying
Creole Fruit Salad (page 57),
   for accompaniment

In a large bowl combine the garlic, thyme, onions, Congo pepper, salt, lime juice, and vinegar. Purée in batches in a blender until smooth.

Place the pork in a nonmetallic bowl. Pour the mixture over the pork and let marinate, covered, in the refrigerator for at least 2 days or preferably 1 week.

Drain the pork and pat dry. Heat the oil in a large skillet over medium heat and sauté the pork cubes, a few at a time, turning often, until browned on all sides (5 to 7 minutes). Drain on paper towels and keep warm in an oven until all are sautéed. Serve with Creole Fruit Salad.

Yield: Makes 6 to 8 servings.

Variations

Some cooks brown the pork slightly and then finish the cooking in a covered casserole dish in a 350 degree F oven for about 30 minutes, adding some water or marinade. For garlic lovers extraordinaire, simmer the marinade until thick and serve it over the pork cubes.

Coconut-Curried Goat

Goat meat, which is not commonly eaten in the United States (except in the Southwest), appears in many West Indian recipes. The Trinis sometimes eat curried goat Jamaican style, but this version with coconut is more customary.

2 tablespoons ghee (clarified butter) or
  vegetable oil
1 onion, finely chopped
2 cloves garlic, minced
3 seasoning peppers or Yellow Wax Hots,
  seeds and stems removed, finely chopped
1 tablespoon grated fresh ginger
2 teaspoons ground coriander
1 teaspoon ground turmeric
1/2 teaspoon freshly ground black pepper
2 teaspoons powdered pure red chiles,
  without spices
1 teaspoon ground cumin
1 1/2 pounds lean goat meat or lamb, cut
  into 1/2-inch cubes
1 1/2 cups water, or more as needed
2 tablespoons coconut cream (page 36)
  (or more, to taste)
Salt, to taste
Chutney (your choice from Chapter 4),
  for accompaniment
Indian Fried Rice (page 89),
  for accompaniment
East Indian bread (your choice from Chapter 9),
  for accompaniment

Heat the ghee in a large skillet over medium heat. Add the onion, garlic, seasoning peppers, and ginger; sauté for 5 minutes, stirring occasionally.

Add the coriander, turmeric, ground pepper, powdered chiles, and cumin; sauté for another 3 minutes, stirring constantly.

Add the meat and cook until browned, stirring occasionally. Add the water and simmer until the meat is tender (about 1 hour), adding more water if the mixture becomes too dry. Stir in the coconut cream and cook for 5 minutes.

Add salt to taste. Serve hot with chutney, fried rice, and breads.

Yield: Makes 4 servings.

Marinated and Rum-Stewed Agouti

Hunters in T&T are particularly fond of the agouti, a large, long-legged, rabbitlike rodent. Rabbit is a good substitute. This method of preparing the game is a combination of African and Portuguese cooking styles and ingredients. Note that the meat must marinate overnight.

2 rear legs from an agouti or rabbit
3 cloves garlic, minced
Freshly ground black pepper, to taste
1/2 cup white rum
4 tablespoons butter
2 tablespoons olive oil
1 Congo pepper or Habanero, left whole
1 teaspoon ground allspice
1 teaspoon minced fresh thyme
1 onion, minced
1 tablespoon minced celery
1/2 teaspoon minced Shadow Bennie
  (culantro) or cilantro
1/4 cup diced carrot
1/2 cup dry white wine
1/2 teaspoon salt
1/2 cup water, or more as needed
Steamed white rice, for accompaniment

Score the agouti legs with a knife, place in a bowl, and add the garlic, ground pepper, and rum. Cover and let marinate overnight in the refrigerator.

Remove the legs and reserve the marinade. In a large saucepan over medium heat, heat the butter and oil. Add the legs and cook until browned, turning occasionally. Add the Congo pepper, allspice, thyme, onion, celery, Shadow Bennie, carrot, wine, salt, and the water. Simmer, covered, for 30 minutes. Add the reserved marinade and simmer until the legs are tender (about 1 hour).

Remove the legs from the sauce. Remove the meat from the bones, cube it, and return it to the pan. Heat, uncovered, until the sauce thickens slightly. Serve hot over the rice.

Yield: Makes 2 servings.

Royal Castle Fried Chicken

This marinated chicken is available all over Trinidad at the Royal Castle restaurants. We've attempted to duplicate the recipe here for people who are not able to visit Trinidad. Marie Permenter serves it with a sweet coleslaw and french fries (called chips). We munched on these while driving all over Trinidad. Mary Jane became addicted to the chicken and began to eat it for breakfast. Note that the chicken must be marinated overnight.

1 chicken (2 1/2 to 3 lb.), cut into 8 pieces
1 bottle (5 oz.) Trinidad Pepper Sauce
    (available at gourmet shops and by mail
    order; see page 107) or more, to taste
2 tablespoons water
Flour, for dredging
Soy or canola oil, for frying

Arrange the chicken in a glass baking dish and pour the sauce over it. Sprinkle it with the water and marinate it overnight in the refrigerator.

Remove the chicken from the marinade and let drain in a colander. Place the chicken pieces in a large plastic bag with the flour. Shake the bag to coat all of the pieces, then fry them in about 1 inch of oil in a large skillet over medium heat, saving the breasts until last since they will take less time. The legs and thighs will take about 8 minutes per side. Do not crowd the chicken—fry it in two batches if necessary.

Drain the chicken on paper towels. Serve immediately with additional pepper sauce.

Yield: Makes 3 or 4 servings.

Twice-Cooked Trinidad Chicken

The number of fast-food shops selling chicken attests to its popularity. Here it is prepared home-style. The phrase "twice-cooked" refers to the browning and then the baking. This chicken dish can also be cooked on top of the stove in a large skillet, but then it becomes "once-cooked" chicken. Note that the chicken must marinate for at least four hours.

1/2 cup All-Purpose Seasoning Mixture
    (page 35)
1 tablespoon Creole Pickle (page 34)
    (optional)
1 cup water
1 chicken (2 1/2 to 3 lb.), cut up
3 tablespoons vegetable oil
2 tablespoons butter
1 tablespoon brown sugar
1 tablespoon Paramin Herb Seasoning
    (page 36)
2 cloves garlic, crushed
1 tablespoon Worcestershire sauce
2 tablespoons tomato paste
2 seasoning peppers or Yellow Wax Hots,
    seeds and stems removed, chopped
2 onions, sliced into rings
1/2 cup dry sherry

In a large bowl combine the seasoning mixture, pickle, and water to make a marinade. Pierce the chicken pieces with a fork and place them in the marinade for at least 4 hours.

Remove the chicken from the marinade and pat dry. In a large skillet over medium heat, heat the oil and butter. Add the brown sugar and cook, stirring constantly, for 1 minute. Add the chicken and sauté until browned (5 to 7 minutes). Add the remaining ingredients, stir well, and cook for about 5 minutes.

Transfer the mixture to a casserole dish and bake, uncovered, in a 350 degree F oven until well browned (30 to 40 minutes). Serve hot.

Yield: Makes 3 or 4 servings.

Chinese Deep-Fried Chicken

We watched this dish being prepared in the kitchen at Johnny's Food Haven and then witnessed it being gobbled up by his lunchtime customers. The only changes we've made for home cooks are to cut up the chicken and to eliminate the monosodium glutamate, which many U.S. cooks avoid anyway.

1 chicken (2 1/2 to 3 lb.), cut into 8 pieces
 and patted dry
4 teaspoons Chinese five-spice powder
Salt and freshly ground black pepper,
 to taste
Vegetable oil, for deep-frying
Island Coleslaw (page 58),
 for accompaniment
Coconut-Stuffed Cush-Cush (page 90),
 for accompaniment

Carefully pull the skin away from the flesh, sprinkle the chicken with 2 teaspoons of the five-spice powder, salt, and ground pepper, and replace the skin. Rub the rest of the five-spice powder on the outside of the chicken pieces, then sprinkle them with salt and ground pepper. Let stand, covered, at room temperature for 1 hour.

Heat the oil in a deep-fryer until a drop of water sprinkled on the surface of the oil evaporates. Add the chicken, a few pieces at time, and deep-fry until lightly browned (about 5 minutes). Lift the chicken pieces out of the fryer with tongs and place them on paper towels.

Allow the oil to come back to temperature, then return the chicken pieces, a few at a time, and fry until golden brown (about 5 minutes more). Drain on paper towels. Serve warm with coleslaw and cush-cush.

Yield: Makes 4 or 5 servings.

Curries for Roti

Roti shops are as common in Trinidad as McDonald's are in the United States. When we visited the Patraj Roti Shop in San Juan, just outside Port of Spain, we tasted nine different kinds of curried fillings for the *roti* bread—fish, beef, chicken, goat, conch, shrimp, liver, duck, and potato. Often, *dhal* (page 56) is spread over the *roti* bread before the filling is added. Below is a typical Trinidadian chicken curry, but virtually any other meat can be substituted. Diced potatoes may be added to any recipe for curried *roti* fillings. Another filling for the *roti* bread is the curried *channa* used to make Doubles (page 41).

1/4 cup vegetable oil
1 onion, chopped
4 cloves garlic, minced
1/4 Congo pepper or Habanero, seeds and
 stem removed, minced
1 chicken (2 1/2 to 3 lb.), cut up
1 tablespoon Paramin Herb Seasoning (page 36)
6 tablespoons Trinidadian Curry Paste (page 35)
 or commercial curry powder
4 cups water
Roti Bread (page 82), for accompaniment
Hot sauce and/or chutney (your choice from
 Chapter 4), for accompaniment

In a large skillet over medium heat, heat the oil. Add the onion, garlic, and Congo pepper; sauté briefly. Add the chicken and cook until browned. Add the herb seasoning and curry paste and cook for 3 minutes, stirring occasionally.

Add the water, stir, reduce the heat to low, and cook, covered, until the chicken is tender (about 45 minutes). Uncover for the last 15 minutes of cooking to allow the sauce to thicken.

Remove the chicken and cut the meat off the bones. Continue to cook the sauce until it is quite thick. Return the chicken to the sauce, stir gently and heat the mixture through.

Fold the curried chicken in the Roti Bread and serve warm, accompanied by hot sauce and chutney.

Yield: Makes 4 to 8 servings, depending on size of bread.

Caribbean Chow Mein

In the United States chow mein is regarded as the epitome of triteness, mostly because it comes in cans, but in T&T it reflects the Chinese influence on the cuisine and is always made from scratch. Note that it lacks cornstarch, so it will not be gooey. Cooks should feel free to use vegetables other than those suggested below.

2 chicken breasts
8 ounces *mein* noodles
3 tablespoons peanut oil
2 cloves garlic, crushed
1 onion, cut into half-rings
1 piece (1 in.) fresh ginger, peeled and slivered
1/2 head cabbage, shredded
1 carrot, slivered
1 bell pepper, seeds and stem removed,
  cut into slices
1 *christophene* (chayote), slivered (optional)
1 small caulifower, broken into florets
2 tablespoons soy sauce, or more as needed
Habanero sauce, to taste (optional)

    Bake the chicken until it is no longer pink. Let it cool, then shred the meat and set aside.

    Boil the noodles in water until soft. Drain and pat them dry. Add 2 tablespoons of the peanut oil to a wok over medium heat; fry the drained noodles until crisp. Remove, drain on paper towels, and keep them warm. Add the remaining tablespoon oil to the wok. Add the shredded chicken, garlic, and onion; stir-fry for 2 minutes.

    Add the remaining ingredients to the wok and stir-fry until the vegetables are cooked but still firm (about 5 minutes). If the mixture is too dry, add more soy sauce (or chicken stock or sherry).

    Serve hot over the reserved noodles.

Yield: Makes 4 servings.

shark-and-bake:
seafood specialties

Seafood is usually an important part of an island's fare. Trinis eat nearly twenty pounds of fish and shellfish per capita every year, making them among the heaviest consumers of seafood in Latin America and the Caribbean. Only about 60 percent of that consumption is fresh or frozen; the remainder is salted, smoked, or canned—a legacy from the days before refrigeration. Salt cod is still popular, as are canned sardines and salmon.

There is a great variety of fresh seafood in T&T, ranging from the familiar offshore fish to the tiny mollusk called chip-chip. Novelist Shiva Naipaul, in his book *The Chip-Chip Gatherers*, described the activity of collecting them. The gatherers were "filling the buckets and basins with the pink and yellow shells which were the size and shape of a long fingernail. Inside each was a sought-after prize: a miniscule kernel of insipid flesh. A full bucket of shells would provide them with a mouthful." Many cooks would disagree with Naipaul's "insipid" description, especially if they were preparing Chip-Chip Chowder (page 53).

Other favorite mollusks are fresh-water oysters, which are collected from mangrove roots in swamps. They used to be sold by Queen's Park Savannah vendors, who would open them and splash them with hot sauce for eager customers. But because of the fear of cholera, this practice has been banned.

Crabs and lobsters commonly appear on T&T restaurant menus. The crabs are usually curried and served with dumplings, or cooked and placed back in the their shells to make Buccoo Crab Backs (page 79). Lobster is served in salads or prepared Chinese style, as in Congo Pepper Lobster Sichuan Style (page 77).

The favored ocean fishes are grouper and king-fish (a large mackerel), but also served regularly are snapper and flying fish, which is a Tobago specialty (page 74). Another fish of choice is shark, which is available from vendors at Maracas Bay.

Shark-and-Bake

This specialty, as served from roadside stands at Maracas Bay, is a kind of T&T version of fish-and-chips. It's relatively easy to duplicate at home; if shark is not available, substitute catfish. If you wish, the shark can be marinated for 2 hours in a mixture of lime juice, chopped onion, minced garlic, minced fresh thyme, and minced Congo pepper.

Juice from 1 lime
1 pound shark meat, cut into pieces 3 to 4
   inches long and 1 inch wide
1 teaspoon minced garlic
2 tablespoons minced chives or green onion tops
1 teaspoon minced fresh thyme
1 teaspoon salt
2 cups flour seasoned with salt and ground
   pepper
Vegetable oil, for frying
2 to 4 Bakes (page 83), for serving
Shadow Bennie Sauce (page 31),
   for accompaniment
Hot sauce (your choice from Chapter 4),
   for accompaniment

Sprinkle the lime juice over the shark and let stand for 5 minutes.

Combine the garlic, chives, thyme, and salt; mix well. Rinse the shark with water and dip first into the garlic mixture, then into the seasoned flour, coating all pieces well.

Heat (over medium heat) sufficient oil to cover the bottom of a large skillet. About 1/8 inch of oil will do here. Add the shark a few pieces at a time and sauté them, turning often, until the fish flakes (about 12 minutes). Drain on paper towels and serve wrapped in Bakes. Sprinkle with Shadow Bennie Sauce and hot sauce.

Yield: Makes 2 to 4 servings.

Wood-Grilled Shark Steaks

Shark and swordfish, or any firm fish that is big enough to have steaks cut from it, lend themselves to grilling. We prefer to grill over hardwood rather than charcoal briquettes; two of the best woods to use are pecan and hickory. Mesquite can be substituted, but it imparts a strong flavor to the fish.

1 cup freshly squeezed lime juice
1/2 teaspoon crushed black pepper
1 teaspoon sherry from Bird Peppers in
    Sherry (page 33) or sherry with a pinch of
    powdered red chiles
4 shark steaks
1/4 cup olive oil
1 teaspoon salt
Creole Fruit Salad (page 57) or
    Ramesar Curried Mango (page 88),
    for accompaniment

In a large bowl combine the lime juice, black pepper, and sherry. Add the shark steaks and marinate them overnight in the refrigerator.

Remove the steaks and pat them dry. Combine the oil and salt and spread over the steaks. Place the steaks in a hinged wire rack (for easy turning) and grill them over hot hardwood coals, taking care that dripping oil does not cause the flames to the burn the steaks. Grill the steaks for about 8 minutes per side, depending on the thickness of the steaks. Serve hot with Creole Fruit Salad.

Yield: Makes 4 servings.

Snapper in Hot Tamarind Sauce

The combination of red snapper with tart tamarind is a tantalizing blend of flavors, especially with just enough Congo pepper to give some heat without being incendiary.

2 tablespoons butter
1 pound red snapper fillets, cut into 1-inch pieces
1 onion, chopped
1 piece (1 in.) fresh ginger, grated
2 cloves garlic, minced
1 bay leaf
1/2 teaspoon minced Congo pepper or Habanero
1/2 teaspoon grated lime zest
1/2 teaspoon ground cinnamon
1/4 cup tamarind pulp
1 tablespoon distilled white vinegar
1 cup water
Steamed rice, for accompaniment
Salad (your choice from Chapter 6),
    for accompaniment

In a large skillet over medium heat, melt 1 tablespoon of the butter. Add the snapper pieces and cook until browned, then remove them and set aside.

Add the remaining tablespoon of butter to the pan; when the butter is melted, add the onion, ginger, and garlic; sauté for 3 minutes. Add the bay leaf, Congo pepper, zest, cinnamon, tamarind, vinegar, and water. Bring to a boil, then reduce heat and simmer, uncovered, until the sauce has thickened slightly (5 to 10 minutes).

Add the reserved fish and simmer, uncovered, for another 15 minutes. Remove and discard the bay leaf. Serve the fish with rice and salad.

Yield: Makes 2 or 3 servings.

Grilled Grouper in Banana Leaves with Garlic-Herb Butter

This tasty dish is served at the Cafe Savannah and was created, like many of the seafood delicacies served there, in a food-storming session consisting of head chef Keith Toby, sous chef Irvine Jackson, and manager Martin Lawrence. Fresh banana leaves are available at Asian and Caribbean markets. Note that the fish must marinate for two to four hours.

Juice of 1 lime
2 cloves garlic, minced
1 teaspoon distilled white vinegar
2 grouper fillets (8 oz. each) or snapper
   or halibut
2 banana leaves
Garlic-Herb Butter (see below), for garnish

    In a large bowl combine the lime juice, garlic, and vinegar. Add the fish and let stand for 2 to 4 hours, turning twice. Meanwhile, prepare the Garlic-Herb Butter and set aside.
    Wrap each fillet tightly in a banana leaf by placing the fillet at one end of the leaf and folding the leaf over, tucking in the sides. Grill the fillet bundles for about 8 minutes, turning once. The fish is done when it flakes easily. Serve it topped with Garlic-Herb Butter.

Yield: Makes 2 servings.

Garlic-Herb Butter
4 tablespoons butter, melted
2 cloves garlic, mashed, then very finely minced
1/2 teaspoon paprika
1/2 teaspoon dried tarragon
1 tablespoon chopped fresh parsley
1/2 teaspoon hot pepper sauce (your choice from
   Chapter 4) or more, to taste

    Combine all of the ingredients in a small bowl and whisk together.

Yield: Makes about 1/4 cup.

Curried Cascadura

Here is a classic T&T dish with one problem—the authentic main ingredient is hard to find! Since the *cascadura*, a primitive Trinidad armored catfish, is generally unavailable outside the islands, substitute farm-raised catfish. Note that the fish fillets must marinate for at least two hours.

2 tablespoons Paramin Herb Seasoning (page 36)
1/4 cup freshly squeezed lime juice
4 catfish fillets
2 tablespoons vegetable oil
1 onion, sliced
1 clove garlic, minced
4 tablespoons Trinidadian Curry Paste
   (page 35)
1 cup coconut milk (page 36)
Breadfruit Oil-Down (page 87),
   for accompaniment
Chutney (your choice from Chapter 4),
   for accompaniment

    In a large bowl combine the herb seasoning and the lime juice. Thoroughly coat the fish fillets, then marinate them for at least 2 hours.
    Heat the oil in a large skillet over medium heat; add the onion and garlic and sauté for 2 minutes. Add the curry paste and cook for another minute. Add the coconut milk and heat through, then add the marinated fillets and coat thoroughly with the sauce. Cover the skillet and simmer until the fillets are flaky (10 to 15 minutes, depending on their thickness).
    Remove the fillets to a serving platter, top with the sauce, and serve with Breadfruit Oil-Down and chutney.

Yield: Makes 4 servings.

Buljol

The name of this salad of shredded salted fish comes from the French *brûle*, meaning burnt, and *geule*, slang for mouth. Since the dish is served at room temperature, the burning is obviously the result of the Congo pepper. Traditionally, *buljol* is served for breakfast or Sunday brunch. Note that salt cod must be soaked and drained for about two hours before using.

8 ounces salt cod or any cooked white
    fish fillet
1 large onion, finely chopped
1 large tomato, finely chopped
1 seasoning pepper or Yellow Wax Hot,
    seeds and stem removed, finely chopped
1 Congo pepper or Habanero, seeds and
    stem removed, finely chopped
Freshly ground black pepper, to taste
3 tablespoons olive oil
Lettuce leaves, for serving
Sliced hard-cooked eggs, for garnish
Sliced avocado, for garnish

If using salt cod, place it in a bowl, cover with boiling water, and let stand for 1 hour. Pour off the water and repeat. Drain the fish, remove any skin or bones, and squeeze out all the water.

Combine the fish with the onion, tomato, seasoning pepper, Congo pepper, ground pepper, and oil; mix well.

Arrange the lettuce leaves on 4 plates, divide the fish mixture evenly over them, garnish with sliced eggs and avocado, and serve.

Yield: Makes 4 servings.

Fried Flying Fish

This dish is a specialty of Tobago, where it is commonly served at restaurants and at the hotels along Courland Bay.

2 eggs
1 1/2 cups flour
1/4 cup minced green onions
2 tablespoons minced fresh parsley
2 teaspoons minced fresh thyme *or*
    1 teaspoon dried thyme
1 teaspoon minced celery leaves
1 teaspoon Worcestershire sauce
Salt, to taste
Freshly ground black pepper, to taste
2 pounds flying fish fillets or other white fish
Vegetable oil, for frying
Tartar sauce, for accompaniment
Hot pepper sauce (your choice from Chapter 4),
    for accompaniment

In a large bowl combine the eggs, flour, onion, parlsey, thyme, celery, Worcestershire, salt, and ground pepper; mix well. Add the fish and let stand for 30 minutes.

Heat (over medium heat) sufficient oil to cover a large skillet to the depth of 1 inch. Add the fish and saute until well browned. Serve with tartar sauce and hot sauce.

Yield: Makes 4 servings.

Braised Kingfish Creole Style

The kingfish, a large mackerel, may be the most popular fish in T&T and is served in many different ways. This recipe reflects the Creole approach of braising the fish in a tomato-based sauce. Serve this dish with Lobster-Stuffed Zabocas (page 58) and your favorite rice dish.

2 tablespoons vegetable oil
4 thick kingfish steaks (or substitute swordfish or tuna)
3 large tomatoes, chopped
1 onion, chopped
1 clove garlic, minced
1 tablespoon Paramin Herb Seasoning (page 36)
2 tablespoons hot sauce (your choice from Chapter 4)
1 tablespoon freshly squeezed lime juice
Water, if needed

In a large skillet over high heat, heat the oil. Add the fish and cook until browned, turning once. Remove the fish and set aside.

Add the remaining ingredients and stir-fry until the tomatoes and onion are soft (about 10 minutes). The sauce should be thick and chunky. If it is soupy, cook a little longer. If it is too dry, add a little water.

Reduce the heat to very low, return the fish to the pan, and cover with the sauce. Cover the pan tightly and cook until the fish flakes easily (15 to 20 minutes, depending on the thickness of the fish). Serve covered with the sauce.

Yield: Makes 4 servings.

Soused Lambie

The word "souse" means to pickle; the term is used loosely here because the conch is flavored with the lime juice rather than being technically pickled. "Lambie" is the Carib Indian word for conch. But no matter what words are used to describe this Creole specialty, its flavor is delightful. Note that the conch should marinate for at least two hours and preferably more than six hours.

2 pounds conch meat
4 cups water
1 tablespoon Paramin Herb Seasoning (page 36)
1 onion, chopped
1 cucumber, peeled and chopped
1/2 Congo pepper or Habanero, seeds and stem removed, minced
1 cup freshly squeezed lime juice
Salt, to taste
1 bunch watercress
1 bell pepper, cut into 8 rings

Pound the conch and chop it into small pieces. In a large saucepan over low heat, combine the conch, water, and herb seasoning; simmer until the conch is tender (at least 1 1/2 hours). Let cool, then drain.

Combine the drained conch with the onion, cucumber, Congo pepper, lime juice, and salt; marinate in the refrigerator for at least 2 hours and preferably for 6 hours or more.

To serve, divide the watercress among 4 plates, place 2 pepper rings on each plate, and top with marinated conch.

Yield: Makes 4 servings.

Variation

For T&T-style ceviche, substitute fresh fish for the conch, but marinate it uncooked in 2 cups freshly squeezed lime juice.

Accras

These fritters, of West African origin, are popular throughout the West Indies and are called stamp-and-go in Jamaica. In Africa they were usually made with black-eyed pea flour, but these days wheat flour is used. The dish is traditionally served with Floats (page 83).

1/2 pound salt cod or any cooked white fish
1 teaspoon active dry yeast
1/4 cup water
1/2 teaspoon sugar
1 cup sifted flour
1 teaspoon baking powder
1/2 teaspoon freshly ground black pepper
1/2 cup milk
1 medium onion, minced
2 seasoning peppers or Yellow Wax Hots,
   seeds and stems removed, minced
1/2 Congo pepper or Habanero, seeds and
   stem removed, minced
1/2 cup minced green onions
1 teaspoon minced fresh thyme *or*
   1/2 teaspoon dried thyme
1 egg, beaten
Vegetable oil, for frying

If using salt cod, soak it in cold water for 30 minutes, rinse 3 times, and shred. Set aside.

Add the yeast to the water, then add the sugar, stir, and let stand for 10 minutes.

Blend together the flour, baking powder, and ground pepper. Add the yeast mixture and the milk and beat with a whisk to make a smooth batter. Add the salt cod and continue to beat briskly. Add the onion, hot chile peppers, green onions, thyme, and egg; again beat briskly. Allow the mixture to stand at room temperature for at least an hour and preferably 2 hours.

Heat (over medium heat) sufficient oil to cover a large skillet to the depth of 1 inch. Drop in the batter a tablespoon at a time. Fry until golden brown, remove, and drain on paper towels. Serve hot.

Yield: Makes about 24 pieces; serves 4 to 6.

Caroni Oysters

The oysters of T&T are small mollusks that live on the mangrove roots in swamps. The public was disappointed when vendors were prohibited from selling this popular fare because of fears of contamination. Any mollusk can be substituted in this recipe, with the normal cautions that accompany the consumption of raw seafood. The oysters can be cooked first, but the flavor is not the same.

1/2 cup catsup
1 tablespoon distilled white vinegar
2 teaspoons Johnny's Food Haven Pepper Sauce
   (page 33) or any commercial Habanero sauce
8 oysters, shucked and drained of juice

Combine the catsup, vinegar, and hot sauce; stir well. Spoon the sauce over the oysters and serve.

Yield: Makes 2 snack-sized servings.

Congo Pepper Lobster Sichuan Style

This lobster dish is a perfect example of merging Chinese cooking techniques with those of the West Indies. Since the dish is so highly spiced, serve it with plain white rice or a pilaf made with Fish Tea (page 51).

2 tablespoons vegetable oil
1 pound cooked shredded lobster meat
3 cloves garlic, minced
1 tablespoon minced fresh ginger
1 teaspoon minced Congo pepper or Habanero
1 tablespoon soy sauce
1 tablespoon rum
1 teaspoon sugar
1/4 cup water
1 teaspoon cornstarch
4 whole green onions

Heat 1 tablespoon of the oil in a wok or skillet over medium heat. Add the lobster and stir-fry for 3 minutes. Remove the lobster and reserve.

Heat the remaining tablespoon of oil in the wok. Add the garlic, ginger, and Congo pepper; stir-fry for 1 minute.

In a small bowl combine the soy sauce, rum, sugar, water, and cornstarch.

Return the lobster to the wok, add the soy sauce mixture and green onions, and cook, stirring often, until thickened (about 3 minutes). Serve hot.

Yield: Makes 4 servings.

Variation
Add snow peas and bean sprouts and cook for an additional 2 minutes.

Curried Lobster

The firm meat of the lobster holds up well in this curry, an example of the East Indian influence in the West Indies. Some cooks add vegetables such as potatoes to this dish, but we prefer to keep it pure and to serve it in the traditional manner—over steamed rice.

3 tablespoons vegetable oil
3 tablespoons butter
3 tablespoons Trinidadian Curry Paste (page 35)
2 onions, chopped
2 cloves garlic, crushed and minced
1 tablespoon grated fresh ginger
3 medium tomatoes, chopped
2 tablespoons freshly squeezed lime juice
2 pounds cooked lobster meat
Steamed white rice, for accompaniment

In a large skillet over medium heat, heat the oil and butter. Add the curry paste, onions, garlic, ginger, tomatoes, and lime juice; cook for about 30 minutes, stirring occasionally. The sauce should be very thick.

Add the lobster, stir well, and simmer for about 10 minutes. Serve over steamed rice.

Yield: Makes 4 servings.

Solimar Crab-Stuffed Coconut Shrimp

This elegant entrée, created by Solimar owner/chef Joe Brown, can be partially prepared ahead of time. Clean the shrimp, stuff them, then refrigerate them until you are ready to dip, roll, and fry them.

Crab Meat Stuffing (see below)
16 to 20 large shrimp, peeled, deveined, and butterflied, tails on
2 egg whites
Large pinch cornstarch
1 cup shredded coconut, fresh or dried, unsweetened
Light sesame oil, for deep-frying (for milder flavor use 1/2 sesame oil and 1/2 canola oil)
Solimar Sweet and Sour Chile Dip (page 34), for accompaniment

Prepare the Crab Meat Stuffing; stuff each shrimp with about 2 tablespoons of the stuffing. Press the shrimp closed as much as possible.

In a small bowl, beat the egg whites and cornstarch with a fork. Dip each shrimp into the mixture, then coat with the coconut to seal in the stuffing.

Heat the oil in a wok or deep fryer to 350 degrees F. A small bread cube should brown nicely when dropped in the oil. Carefully lower several shrimp into the hot oil. Do not crowd. Fry for 1 to 2 minutes per side. Drain on a paper towel and test one of the shrimp for doneness. If it is done, proceed with remaining shrimp in small batches, keeping each batch warm in the oven as they drain on paper towels.

Serve at once with the chile dip.

Yield: Makes 4 servings.

Crab Meat Stuffing
2 cups cooked crab meat
1 cup small cooked shrimp
2 cloves garlic
1 teaspoon grated fresh ginger
2 teaspoons minced cilantro
1 or 2 small hot chile peppers, such as *piquins* or *serranos*
Salt and freshly ground pepper, to taste
1/4 cup finely diced water chestnuts

In a food processor combine the crab meat, shrimp, garlic, ginger, cilantro, hot peppers, salt, and ground pepper. Blend until smooth. Stir in the water chestnuts and mix thoroughly.

Yield: Makes about 3 1/2 cups.

Chow Har Look

This stir-fried shrimp with ginger in banana catsup is a Chinese-style treatment of shrimp that is popular in T&T. Some versions of this dish call for commercial tomato catsup; others call for tomato sauce. We prefer to use one of the more exotic catsups on the market.

1/2 cup olive oil
2 tablespoons minced fresh ginger
2 cloves garlic, minced
2 pounds cleaned medium shrimp
3/4 cup banana catsup
2 tablespoons rum or sherry
1 teaspoon sugar
1 tablespoon Tamarind-Mango Chutney (page 38)
1 tablespoon cornstarch mixed with
   4 tablespoons water
Steamed white rice, for accompaniment

Heat the oil in a wok over medium heat, add the ginger and garlic, and stir-fry for 1 minute. Add the shrimp and stir-fry for 5 minutes. Add the catsup, rum, sugar, chutney, and cornstarch mixture; stir-fry until the sauce thickens (6 to 8 minutes more). Serve hot over rice.

Yield: Makes 6 servings.

Buccoo Crab Backs

This tasty entrée, which also can be served as an appetizer, is named after Buccoo Reef off the west coast of Tobago, famous for fish watching. Crab backs are popular fare in the shoreside restaurants there.

4 tablespoons butter
1 tablespoon All-Purpose Seasoning Mixture
   (page 35)
1 onion, chopped
3 cloves garlic, minced
2 tablespoons chopped celery
1 tablespoon chopped green onion tops
1 pound cooked crab meat, chopped
1 cup dried bread crumbs
6 crab backs (shells), cleaned
Minced red bell pepper, for garnish
Sliced lime, for garnish

Melt the butter in a large skillet over medium heat. Add the seasoning mixture, onion, garlic, celery, and green onion; sauté for 5 minutes. Add the crab meat and sauté for another 5 minutes. Remove the pan from the heat and stir in the bread crumbs.

Stuff the crab backs with the crab mixture, place on a baking sheet, and bake in a 350 degree F oven for 20 minutes. Garnish with bell pepper and lime and serve.

Yield: Makes 3 entrée servings, 6 appetizer servings.

Curried Crab and Dumplings

Patricia Blake, a cook at Johnny's Food Haven, invited us to watch her prepare this dish in the restaurant's tiny kitchen. She used the traditional whole blue crabs and cooked them in the curry mixture with additional coconut milk. We have adjusted the recipe to avoid the tedious cracking of the crabs. The dumplings are very heavy (a "bellyfull" in Trini slang) and end up being chewy. Those who are not dumpling fans can serve the curried crab over white rice.

2 tablespoons vegetable oil
2 tablespoons West Indian Masala (page 34) or
  Trinidadian Curry Paste (page 35)
1 clove garlic, minced
1/2 cup chopped celery
1 onion, chopped
3 green onions (including some green tops),
  chopped
3 seasoning peppers or Yellow Wax Hots,
  seeds and stems removed, chopped
2 tomatoes, chopped
4 cups coconut milk (page 36)
1 to 1 1/2 pounds cooked crab meat
Salt, to taste
2 tablespoons butter

In a large saucepan over medium heat, heat the oil until hot. Add the masala, garlic, celery, onion, green onions, seasoning peppers, and tomatoes; sauté for at least 5 minutes, stirring constantly.

Add the coconut milk, increase the heat to high and bring to a boil, then reduce the heat to low and simmer for about 15 minutes for the flavors to blend.

Meanwhile, prepare the dumplings. Add the cooked and drained dumplings to the curry mixture along with the crab meat. Taste for salt, add the butter, and heat until thickened (6 to 8 minutes). Serve hot.

Yield: Makes 4 to 6 servings.

Flour Dumplings

2 cups flour, or more as needed
1/2 teaspoon salt
3 teaspoons baking powder
2 tablespoons vegetable shortening
2/3 cup milk

Sift the flour, salt, and baking powder together into a large bowl. Add the shortening and work into the flour mixture with a fork until thoroughly mixed. Add the milk gradually and mix until soft dough forms.

Turn the dough out onto a floured board and knead for about 1 minute, adding more flour if necessary to prevent sticking. Roll out the dough to about 1/2 inch thick. Cut into pieces about 2 by 3 inches. Cook in boiling salted water for 10 to 15 minutes, then drain.

buss-up-shut:
breads and
accompaniments

Mostly because of the East Indian influence on the cuisine of T&T, breads are ubiquitous on the two islands, particularly Trinidad. A number of names are given to East Indian breads that are cooked on a griddle: *roti* (the generic Hindi word for bread), *paratha*, *chapatti*, *dosti*, and *sada*. All are a combination of flour, baking powder, salt, and water; they differ from the breads of India only in the addition of baking powder. The extremely thin dough made with these ingredients is usually cooked on a large, flat griddle called a *tawa*.

We watched women preparing breads for *roti* at the Patraj Roti Shop in San Juan and were amazed at their ability to make the breads so thin. It was quite an operation in the bread kitchen, with as many as six women working at various stages of production and assistants using carts to wheel the bread to the serving area, where it was combined with as many as nine different curried fillings.

Fried breads, called floats, bakes, or *bara*, also appear with great frequency in the Trini diet. Baked breads, such as hops and Banana Coconut Bread (page 84), are less common but no less tasty. Two interesting hybrid breads are Cornmeal-Coconut Coo-Coo (page 86), a Creole favorite that is nearly a custard, and Sahina (page 86), which is part fritter.

Curried vegetables are popular accompaniments in T&T, and we have uncovered some tasty recipes for currying potatoes, cabbage, mangoes, and cauliflower. Other accompaniments are rice dishes, which are usually simple variations on steamed or boiled rice with some spices added. We have included a more imaginative recipe, Indian Fried Rice (page 89).

Plantains, yams, cassava, and breadfruit are commonly served on the side; one particularly interesting recipe is Breadfruit Oil-Down (page 87).

Buss-Up-Shut and Roti Bread

When any of the griddle breads are ripped apart for dipping into curries, they are called buss-up-shut, vernacular for "burst-up-shirt," because they resemble torn cloth. When left whole, the breads are stuffed with curried meat, seafood, or vegetables and rolled up in the manner of a burrito.

3 cups flour
3 teaspoons baking powder
1/2 teaspoon salt
1 cup water
Vegetable oil, as needed

Sift together the flour, baking powder, and salt. Add the water and mix to form a dough. Knead, then let stand for 30 minutes. Knead again and divide into 4 balls.

On a floured board roll out each ball as thin as possible—to a diameter of 8 to 10 inches.

In a large skillet or griddle over medium heat, heat sufficient oil to coat the pan. Cook each *roti* for about 1 1/2 minutes per side, drizzling additional oil onto each side as it cooks. Remove carefully and drain on paper towels. *Rotis* can be left whole for stuffing or torn up for dipping.

Yield: Makes *roti* breads.

Floats

This simple, fried yeast bread is traditionally served with Accras (page 76). The name probably derived from the tendency of the bread rounds to float on top of the hot oil while frying.

1 teaspoon active dry yeast
3/4 cup warm water
1 teaspoon sugar
1/2 teaspoon salt
3 1/2 cups sifted flour
3 tablespoons butter, melted
Vegetable oil, as needed

Combine the yeast with 1/4 cup of the water and let stand for 5 minutes, then add the remaining 1/2 cup water, sugar, salt, and flour. Beat well to form dough. Turn out onto a floured board and knead until smooth. Shape into a ball.

Place the ball of dough in a greased bowl, cover with a cloth, and set the bowl in a warm place until the dough has doubled in size. Shape into 6 small balls and set aside to rise again for about 30 minutes.

Roll out the balls into thin rounds. In a large skillet over medium heat, heat sufficient oil to coat the pan. Cook the dough rounds until browned. Drain on paper towels and serve warm.

Yield: Makes 6 pieces.

Bakes

This is the bread that is served with shark to make the famous Maracas Bay Shark-and-Bake (page 70). This dish is simple and quick to prepare.

2 cups flour
2 teaspoons baking powder
1 teaspoon salt
8 tablespoons butter
1 teaspoon sugar
Water, as needed
Vegetable oil, for frying

In a large bowl, sift together the flour, baking powder, and salt. Cut in the butter and add the sugar; mix with a fork until well combined. Add enough water to make a dough and knead gently.

Cut the dough into 4 to 6 pieces (depending on the desired size of the bakes) and roll each piece into a ball. Let stand for a few minutes.

Flatten the balls of dough to about 1/4 inch thick. In a large skillet over medium heat, heat sufficient oil to coat the pan. Cook the dough until browned. Drain on paper towels and serve warm.

Yield: Makes 4 to 6 pieces.

Hops

This traditional, simple bread is baked instead of fried. It is often served with Fish Tea (page 51). The origin of the name is obscure.

2 1/2 cups warm water
2 teaspoons sugar
1 tablespoon active dry yeast
8 cups flour, or more as needed
2 teaspoons salt

Place the water in a large bowl, add the sugar, and stir until dissolved. Add the yeast, stir until dissolved, and let stand for 10 minutes.

Stir in the flour and salt and mix well. Turn the dough out onto a floured board and knead for 8 to 10 minutes, adding more flour if necessary to make a stiff dough. Transfer to a greased bowl, cover with a cloth, and allow to rise for 25 minutes.

Punch the down dough, form into 12 balls, and place on greased baking sheets. Cover with a damp cloth and let rise until doubled in size (1 to 2 hours).

Bake in a 400 degree F oven for 20 minutes. Serve warm.

Yield: Makes 12 pieces.

Banana Coconut Bread

This easy-to-make, versatile bread can be served as soon as it is cool enough to slice. Try it for sandwiches, as a sweet with coffee, or even as a dessert. It is good plain or embellished with cream cheese or butter. It freezes well.

3/4 cup sugar
1/4 cup shortening
2 eggs
1 cup mashed banana
1/2 cup shredded coconut, fresh or dried, unsweetened
2 cups flour
2 teaspoons baking powder
1/2 teaspoon salt
1/4 teaspoon baking soda
1 cup chopped pecans or walnuts (optional)

In a large bowl combine the sugar, shortening, and eggs; beat until light and fluffy. Add the mashed banana and coconut and stir to combine.

Sift the flour with the baking powder, salt, and baking soda. Add to the banana mixture and stir until smooth. Add the nuts if desired and stir again.

Pour the batter into a greased 9- by 5- by 3-inch loaf pan. Bake in a 350 degree F oven until a cake tester comes out clean (60 to 70 minutes). Remove from the oven and allow to cool in the pan. Use 2 spatulas to remove the loaf from the pan; let it finish cooling on a wire rack. Slice and serve, or wrap in aluminum foil and store in the freezer.

Yield: Makes 1 loaf.

Split Pea Bara Bread

This is one version of the bread used to make doubles (page 41). (Yeast Bara Bread is the other version.) To keep the dough from sticking to your hands, keep them lightly floured, or dip your hands in water as you shape each piece of *bara*. Some recipes for this bread contain garlic and some do not; finding a consensus on the best recipe for this bread would be like trying to get Texans to agree on the best recipe for chili con carne.

1 cup ground split pea flour (see Note)
1/2 cup all-purpose flour
3 teaspoons baking powder
1/2 teaspoon salt
1/4 teaspoon ground cumin
1/2 teaspoon ground turmeric
1 clove garlic, minced
1 Congo pepper or Habanero, seeds and
  stem removed, minced (optional)
1/4 cup lukewarm water, or more as needed
Canola or soy oil, for frying

In a large bowl combine the flours, baking powder, salt, cumin, and turmeric. Add the garlic and Congo pepper. Add the water and mix thoroughly. The dough should be soft; if it is too thick, add more water by tablespoons. Be sure to mix thoroughly after each addition of water so that the dough does not become sticky. Cover and let stand until the dough starts to puff up (30 to 45 minutes).

In a small skillet over medium heat, add the oil to a depth of 1 inch and heat. Pull off 12 to 16 generous tablespoons of dough; flatten with your hands or gently roll with a rolling pin until about 1/4 inch thick and 3 to 4 inches in diameter.

Fry the rounds, one at a time, in hot oil until lightly browned (30 to 60 seconds on each side). The oil should be about 1/2 inch deep. It's best to try one first for timing before frying the rest. Drain on paper towels and keep warm until serving.

Yield: Makes 12 to 16 *baras*.

Note: If split pea flour is not available at your local natural foods store, buy dried split peas and soak them overnight in water. Drain off the liquid and grind the peas in a blender, adding back some water if necessary. The peas can also be boiled in water until barely soft and then ground in the blender.

Yeast Bara Bread

Here is the other version of the bread used to make doubles.

2 cups all-purpose flour
1/2 teaspoon salt
1 teaspoon ground turmeric
1/2 teaspoon ground cumin
1/3 cup warm water, or more as needed
1/4 teaspoon sugar
1 teaspoon active dry yeast
Canola or soy oil, for frying

In a large bowl combine the flour, salt, turmeric, and cumin; set aside.

Pour the water into a small bowl and sprinkle with the sugar and yeast. Let stand until the yeast has dissolved (about 5 minutes).

Make a well in the flour mixture and pour in the yeast mixture. Mix thoroughly; if the dough seems dry, add a few more tablespoons of water. Cover with a damp cloth and let rise for 1 hour.

Punch down the dough and let stand for 10 minutes. Meanwhile, heat the oil in a large skillet over medium heat.

Pull off 12 to 16 generous tablespoons of dough and flatten into rounds 4 to 5 inches in diameter with your hands or a rolling pin. If the dough sticks to your hands, flour or dampen them with water.

Fry the rounds, one at a time, in hot oil until lightly browned (30 to 60 seconds on each side), turning once. The oil should be about 1/2 inch deep. Drain on paper towels and keep warm until serving.

Yield: Makes 12 to 16 *baras*.

Cornmeal-Coconut Coo-Coo

Half-bread and half-custard, this traditional Creole dish once had tomatoes, chives, and onions added to it. More recent recipes use just okras, which thicken the mixture considerably. Serve coo-coo as an accompaniment to Callaloo (page 50) or Sancoche (page 55).

4 okras, thinly sliced
2 cups coconut milk (page 36), or more
  as needed
1 tablespoon butter
Salt, to taste
1 cup cornmeal

In a large saucepan over medium heat, combine the okras, coconut milk, butter, and salt. Bring to a boil, then reduce the heat and cook until the okras are soft (about 10 minutes).

Gradually add the cornmeal, stirring constantly. Cook for 3 minutes, continuing to stir to prevent sticking. If the mixture becomes too thick, add a bit more coconut milk.

Pour the mixture into a greased 4- by 6-inch (or equivalent size) pan. After the mixture cools and sets, cut it into squares and serve.

Yield: Makes 4 to 6 servings.

Sahina

We cooked this East Indian side dish under the careful supervision of Nancy Ramesar. These tasty treats freeze well and can be quickly reheated in a conventional or microwave oven.

1/2 cup all-purpose flour
2 1/4 cups split pea flour or cooked mashed
  split peas (see Note)
2 tablespoons baking powder
1 1/2 teaspoons salt
2 cups water
1 seasoning pepper or Yellow Wax Hot,
  seeds and stem removed, minced
1 cup chopped raw *dasheen* or
  spinach leaves
1/2 cup soy or canola oil
Ramesar Mango Chutney (page 37),
  for accompaniment

In a large bowl combine the flours, baking powder, and salt; mix well. Add the water, seasoning pepper, and *dasheen* and mix again. The mixture should be the consistency of a heavy pancake batter.

Heat 2 tablespoons of the oil in a large skillet over medium heat. When hot (a drop of water sprinkled on surface will sizzle and evaporate), drop in 1/4 cup batter and fry until golden brown, turning once. Drain the bread on paper towels and keep warm in the oven. Add more oil and repeat until all batter is used. Serve with chutney.

Yield: Makes 6 servings.

Note: If split pea flour is not available, use dried split peas and soak them overnight in water. Drain off the liquid and grind the peas in a blender, adding back some water if necessary. The peas can also be boiled in water until barely soft and then ground in the blender.

Spiced Yogurt Potatoes

Here is an accompaniment with a distinct East Indian influence. Although curry powder or paste is not used, the potatoes are considered curried in the sense that they are heavily spiced.

1 pound cooked potatoes, peeled and diced
2 cups plain yogurt
1/2 teaspoon ground cumin
1/2 teaspoon powdered red chile
1/2 teaspoon ground coriander
1/2 teaspoon ground turmeric
3 tablespoons vegetable oil
1/4 teaspoon mustard seeds
1/4 teaspoon cumin seeds
1 piece (1 in.) fresh ginger, peeled and
  chopped
Water, as needed
Shadow Bennie (*culantro*) or cilantro leaves,
  for garnish

In a large bowl combine the potatoes, yogurt, cumin, powdered chile, coriander, and turmeric; mix well and set aside.

Heat the oil in a large skillet over medium heat. Add the mustard seeds and cook until they start to pop. Add the cumin seeds and ginger and fry for 2 minutes.

Add the reserved potato mixture, reduce the heat to low, and simmer for 5 minutes. Add water if the mixture becomes too dry. Serve hot, garnished with Shadow Bennie.

Yield: Makes 4 servings.

Breadfruit Oil-Down

There is a modest debate in the West Indies about the origin of this dish, with some experts attributing it to Barbados rather than to T&T. The phrase "oil-down" refers to a dish cooked in coconut milk until all the milk is absorbed, leaving a bit of coconut oil in the bottom of the pan. Early recipes call for a mixture of salted pig's tail, pig's feet (trotters), and salt beef, but in today's kitchen it's much easier (and less salty) to use ham.

1/2 pound smoked ham, diced
1 tablespoon vegetable oil
1 large onion, minced
2 seasoning peppers or Yellow Wax Hots,
  seeds and stems removed, finely chopped
1 clove garlic, minced
1/2 Congo pepper or Habanero, seeds and
  stem removed
1 bunch green onions, including green
  tops, finely chopped
2 teaspoons minced fresh thyme *or*
  1 teaspoon dried thyme
4 cups coconut milk (page 36)
1 large breadfruit, peeled and cut into 8
  sections (or substitute canned)
Salt and ground pepper, to taste

Place the ham in a large saucepan, cover with water, and bring to a boil. Reduce the heat and simmer until the ham is tender (20 to 30 minutes), skimming off any foam that rises. Drain the ham and set aside.

In a large skillet over medium heat, heat the oil. Add the onion, seasoning peppers, garlic, Congo pepper, green onions, and thyme; sauté for about 5 minutes, stirring constantly. Add the coconut milk and heat briefly, then add the breadfruit, reserved ham, salt, and ground pepper. Reduce the heat to low and simmer, covered, until the breadfruit has absorbed all the coconut milk (about 30 minutes). Serve hot.

Yield: Makes 6 to 8 servings.

Curried Cauliflower
à la Trinidad

Since virtually every vegetable grown in Trinidad is cooked in a curry sauce at one time or another, you can substitute carrots, potatoes, okra, fresh peas, or green beans for the cauliflower, or mix any of these with it.

2 pounds cauliflower, trimmed, washed,
  and broken into small florets
1/4 cup canola oil
1/2 teaspoon black mustard seeds
1/2 teaspoon cumin seeds
2 1/2 tablespoons minced fresh ginger
1/4 cup finely chopped onion
Pinch salt
1/2 teaspoon ground turmeric
1 medium tomato, finely chopped
1/2 Congo pepper or Habanero, seeds and
  stem removed, finely chopped
1/2 teaspoon ground cumin
1/2 teaspoon sugar
4 large leaves Shadow Bennie (*culantro*),
  chopped, *or* 3 tablespoons chopped fresh
  cilantro

Parboil the cauliflower in rapidly boiling water for 1 minute, then drain and set aside.

Heat the oil in a large heavy skillet over medium heat. Add the mustard seeds, cumin seeds, ginger, and onion; cook for 1 minute, stirring constantly. Add the salt and turmeric and cook for another 3 to 4 minutes, stirring constantly. Add the reserved cauliflower, tomato, Congo pepper, ground cumin, sugar, and Shadow Bennie; reduce the heat to low and slowly simmer until the cauliflower is thoroughly coated but still crispy (about 5 minutes). Serve hot.

Yield: Makes 6 to 8 servings.

Ramesar Curried Mango

Nancy Ramesar includes the mango seed in this recipe because she likes to nibble the pulp off it. Nancy uses the famous Chief brand of *amchar masala*, but some good substitutes are offered in Chapter 4.

4 half-ripe mangoes, skin on
2 tablespoons vegetable oil
2 cloves garlic, mashed
1 cup water, or more as needed
2 tablespoons West Indian Masala (page 34) or
  commercial curry powder
1 teaspoon sugar, if needed

Scrub the mangoes thoroughly and cut into 2-inch slices, leaving some pulp on the seeds. Set aside.

In a large heavy casserole dish over medium heat, heat the oil. Add the garlic, the water, and *masala* and cook for 2 to 3 minutes. Add the reserved mango slices and stir to coat. Reduce the heat, cover, and simmer until mangoes are tender (30 to 40 minutes). Check about halfway through cooking time and add more water if the mixture is too dry. Taste the mixture at the end of the cooking time; if it is too sour, add sugar. Serve hot.

Yield: Makes 6 to 8 servings as a side dish.

Curried Cabbage and Potatoes

As Nancy Ramesar cleaned the cabbage and chopped it into wedges for this dish, she sang Irish folk songs—and also sang bits of culinary information: "Remember, love, anything green and leafy is called 'bush.'" It was a lovely afternoon and evening of cooking in their airy house off Lady Chancellor Road, high above Port of Spain.

1 teaspoon vegetable oil
1 tablespoon Nancy's Seasoning Paste (page 36)
1 teaspoon Trinidadian Curry Paste (page 35)
1 small cabbage (1 to 1 1/2 pounds),
  washed and cut into wedges
2 cups diced potatoes
Water, if needed

In a heavy skillet or casserole dish over high heat, heat the oil. Add the seasoning paste and curry paste and cook for about 30 seconds. Add the cabbage and potatoes and cook for another minute. Reduce the heat to low, cover the pot, and simmer until the potatoes are firm but easily pierced with a fork (15 to 20 minutes). Add a little water if necessary, but remember that cabbage will release some moisture as it cooks. Serve hot.

Yield: Makes 4 to 6 servings.

Indian Fried Rice

This side dish, which resembles a pilaf, can be cooked on top of the stove or baked. The key to the flavor is the mixture of spices, which reflects the East Indian influence in T&T cookery.

1/4 cup vegetable oil or ghee (clarified butter)
1 large onion, minced
2 cups long-grain white rice
1/2 teaspoon ground cloves
1/2 teaspoon ground cardamom
1/2 teaspoon ground cinnamon
1/2 teaspoon ground cumin
4 cups water

In a large skillet over medium heat, heat the oil. Add the onion and sauté until soft. Add the rice and sauté until golden brown. Stir in the cloves, cardamom, cinnamon, and cumin. Add the water and stir again. Cover the pan, reduce the heat to low, and cook until all water is absorbed (about 20 minutes). Remove from the heat, stir, and let stand for 5 to 10 minutes before serving.

Yield: Makes 6 to 8 servings.

Variations
To bake the rice, after stirring in the spices and the water, transfer the rice mixture to a ceramic baking dish and bake, covered, in a 350 degree F oven for about 40 minutes. Remove the cover during the last 10 minutes of cooking for crispier rice. Chicken or beef stock may be substituted for the water to match the rice to a main dish. For Hot Curried Fried Rice, substitute Trinidadian Curry Paste (page 35) for the spices and add 1 tablespoon minced Congo pepper or Habanero.

Sautéed Cassava

We first tried this dish at Johnny's Food Haven. Trinis really like their cassava, and Johnny said he sells about 150 pounds of it every week. This brown root can be found at Latin markets and even in large supermarkets, where it's sometimes labeled yuca. Breadfruit or yams may be substituted. In any case, this is a fine accompaniment to a Caribbean dinner.

2 pounds cassava, peeled and cut into
  2-inch rounds
2 tablespoons vegetable oil
2 tablespoons butter
2 onions, chopped
1/2 cup chopped celery
1 small shallot, chopped
1/2 cup coarsely chopped carrot
1/4 cup chopped fresh parsley
2 cloves garlic, minced
1/2 teaspoon salt
1/2 teaspoon freshly ground black pepper
1/4 cup water

Boil the cassava in water to cover until soft (30 to 45 minutes). Drain and keep warm.

In a large skillet over medium heat, heat the oil and butter. Add the onions, celery, shallot, carrot, parsley, garlic, salt, and ground pepper; sauté until well blended (about 5 minutes). Add the water and cook for another 2 minutes. Pour the mixture over the warm cassava and serve.

Yield: Makes 6 to 8 servings.

Coconut-Stuffed Cush-Cush

The terms "sweet potato" and "yam" are often used interchangeably, since these two tubers look similar. However, they are different species. Yams, in fact, have more sugar than sweet potatoes but less vitamins A and C. In T&T yams are called cush-cush. Despite all the confusion, sweet potatoes can be substituted in this recipe.

2 yams, scrubbed
2 tablespoons grated coconut, fresh or dried,
  unsweetened
3 tablespoons beer
4 tablespoons butter, melted
2 teaspoons ground allspice

Bake the yams in a 350 degree F oven until they can be easily pierced with a knife (about 1 hour).

Cut the yams in half and carefully remove the pulp, taking care not to break the skins. In a large bowl, combine the pulp with the coconut, beer, and butter; mash well. Return the mixture to the skins, sprinkle with allspice, and place under the broiler until browned. Serve hot.

Yield: Makes 4 servings.

tooLum:
sweets and desserts

The numerous refreshment stands and pastry shops all over the islands reflect the sweet tooth of the Trinis, who in 1971 had an annual per-capita consumption of more than ninety pounds of sugar! Sylvia Hunt, a noted Trinidadian cookbook author, has observed: "Sweet making in Trinidad and Tobago is inextricably bound up with sugar-cane production and cocoa production, two crops which have had a profound effect on our history."

Hunt pointed out that historically the raw materials of candy were exported to England, where large industries transformed the sugar and cocoa into jellies, candies, and chocolates, which "were then exported back to us at extremely high prices which only the well-to-do could afford." The only recourse for the poor people was to create their own sweets at home, and they did so very well.

There is an astounding variety of sweets in T&T, and candies and desserts are eaten at all times of the day. Beyond a simple love of sweets, there are other reasons for the popularity of candies. An East Indian legend holds that sugar cane juice improves sexual performance. Sweets also symbolize success to the East Indian population of Trinidad.

West Indian sweets are flavored with tropical island spices from all over the world, such as cinnamon, nutmeg, and vanilla. As might be expected, many of the sweets and desserts originate from locally grown products, such as coconuts and fruits. Trinis are conspicuous consumers of fruits, especially mangoes, oranges, bananas, grapefruit, and papayas. Imported apples, pears, peaches, and grapes are eaten as Christmas treats.

Some of the desserts, such as Joe Brown's Double Chocolate Mousse (page 97), are incredibly rich. Others, such as Mango-Fig Ice Cream (page 96) and Trini Tropical Trifle (page 99), are laden with fruits and are not as rich.

Although we had always heard that there was a famous Trinidadian chocolate cake or pudding named after Pitch Lake, none of our Trinidadian friends had ever heard of it. We later discovered that there is both a cake and a pudding, but they are Bajan dishes that originated in Barbados, not T&T.

Toolum

In the early part of the twentieth century, sweet vendors would comb the streets of T&T towns and villages, selling candies by spinning a wheel. For a penny, a customer spun the wheel and received the number of candies indicated when the wheel stopped—up to fifty. *Toolum*, one of the earliest T&T candies, was undoubtedly supplied by such vendors.

2 cups firmly packed brown sugar
1/2 cup molasses
5 cups grated coconut, fresh or dried, unsweetened
2 tablespoons crushed dried orange zest
1 tablespoon grated fresh ginger
Grated coconut, for topping

In a large saucepan over low heat, melt the brown sugar and cook until golden brown, stirring constantly. Add the molasses while continuing to stir. Add the coconut, zest, and ginger. Reduce the heat to very low and cook until the mixture separates smoothly from the bottom and sides of the pan, stirring constantly.

Remove the pan from the heat and allow the mixture to cool. Drop spoonfuls of the mixture into little cones onto aluminum foil or a lightly oiled baking sheet. Sprinkle each cone with grated coconut. Allow to cool. Serve or store in an airtight container.

Yield: Makes about 30 candies.

Cassava Pone

This traditional island dessert can also be made with sweet potatoes, yams, pumpkin, or any combination of these ingredients. Brown sugar can be used instead of granulated sugar. Sometimes raisins, ground nutmeg, and ground ginger are added.

2 cups grated cassava (yuca)
1 cup grated coconut, fresh or dried,
   unsweetened
1 cup granulated sugar
1 teaspoon ground cinnamon
4 tablespoons butter, melted
1/2 cup evaporated milk
1 teaspoon vanilla extract

In a large bowl combine all ingredients. Transfer to a greased 8-inch square baking dish and bake in a 350 degree F oven until browned and firm to the touch (about 45 minutes). Cut into small squares and serve.

Yield: Makes 8 servings.

Chip-Chip

Why this coconut candy has the same name as an edible mollusk is anyone's guess. It is also the name of a sliding dance step performed during Carnival, so the expression really gets around. Sometimes this simple candy is tinted with a little food coloring to make pastel shades.

4 cups water
2 cups shredded and minced fresh coconut
2 cups sugar
1/4 teaspoon cream of tartar
Food coloring (optional)

Bring 2 cups of the water to a boil, add the coconut, and continue boiling until the water evaporates, taking care not to burn the coconut. Remove from the heat and drain the coconut.

Make a sugar syrup by bringing the remaining 2 cups water to a boil, adding the sugar gradually, and cooking over low heat until thick.

Add the drained coconut and cream of tartar to the sugar syrup; cook until the coconut begins to hold together and the mixture is thick and creamy. Add the food coloring, if desired.

Remove from the heat. Drop spoonfuls of the coconut mixture onto a smooth surface, such as glass or enamel. Let the candy stand until it dries, then serve or store in an airtight jar or tin.

Yield: Makes 25 to 30 candies.

Tamarind Balls

This favorite sweet is a combination of tart tamarind, sugar, and salt. Sometimes even a bit of Congo pepper is added to really confuse the tongue!

2 cups tamarind pulp
2 cups sugar, or more as needed
1 tablespoon salt

Combine all of the ingredients and stir. If the mixture is not firm enough to roll into balls, add more sugar.

Shape the mixture into balls and roll in additional sugar. Wrap the balls in waxed paper until ready to eat.

Yield: Makes 8 to 10 servings.

Cocoa and Cashew Fudge

This candy for chocolate lovers combines two T&T naturals, cocoa (chocolate) and cashew nuts. In the Trinidad countryside, you can see "cocoa houses," with roofs but no sides, which are used to dry the hanging cocoa pods.

3 tablespoons unsalted butter
3 tablespoons cocoa powder
1 1/2 cups sweetened condensed milk
1 pound confectioners' sugar
2 cups ground roasted unsalted cashews

In a large saucepan over medium heat, melt the butter. Remove the pan from the heat and stir in the cocoa powder to make a paste. Stir in the milk.

Combine the sugar and cashews; add to the cocoa mixture and stir to combine.

Turn the mixture onto a smooth surface, such as glass or marble, and knead well until smooth. Shape the mixture into a block approximately 1 inch thick; cut the block into small squares. Let the fudge stand, covered with a cloth, until set (about a day). Serve or store in an airtight container.

Yield: Makes 8 or more servings.

Allspice Pumpkin Bread

Pumpkins, which are actually a variety of winter squash, are so popular in T&T that they show up in dishes of every possible kind. This dessert bread can be served plain or topped with whipped cream and dusted with ground allspice.

1 cup firmly packed brown sugar
1/2 cup granulated sugar
1 cup cooked butternut squash or canned pumpkin
1/2 cup vegetable oil
2 eggs
2 cups sifted flour
1 teaspoon baking soda
1/2 teaspoon salt
2 teaspoons ground allspice
1/4 teaspoon ground ginger
1 cup raisins
1/2 cup chopped unsalted cashews or walnuts
1/4 cup water

In a large bowl combine the sugars, squash, oil, and eggs; beat until well blended. In another large bowl combine the flour, baking soda, salt, allspice, and ginger; add to the squash mixture and stir to combine. Stir in the raisins, nuts, and the water until well blended.

Pour the batter into a well-greased 9- by 5- by 3-inch loaf pan. Bake in a 350 degree F oven until a cake tester comes out clean (about 70 minutes). Turn the loaf out onto a wire rack to cool before serving.

Yield: Makes 1 loaf, about 8 servings.

Mango Mousse

Interesting methods of using fruits seem to crop up often in Trini recipes. This particular dessert calls for mangoes, but nearly any fruit will work. Recommended are pineapple, passion fruit, or guava. Note that the mixture must be refrigerated for at least four hours before serving.

1 tablespoon powdered unflavored gelatin
1 1/4 cups water
1/2 cup sugar
2 cups mango pulp, puréed in a blender
1/3 cup freshly squeezed lime juice
1 cup whipping cream plus whipped cream,
   for garnish
2 tablespoons Curaçao liqueur
Thin slice fresh mango, for garnish

Combine the gelatin and 1/4 cup of the water.

Bring the remaining 1 cup water to a boil; add the sugar and stir until it is dissolved. Remove from the heat, add the gelatin mixture, and let cool.

In the container of a blender, combine the mango pulp, lime juice, and the gelatin mixture. Purée, then refrigerate until partially set.

Whip the 1 cup cream until peaks form. Add the Curaçao and beat well; fold into the mango mixture and refrigerate for at least 4 hours. Serve garnished with a dab of whipped cream and a mango slice.

Yield: Makes 6 to 8 servings.

Sewain

Vermicelli, an ingredient not usually associated with Indian cooking, is the base of this unusual East Indian dessert. Also called *sooji ka halva*, it may be eaten either hot or cold.

2 tablespoons butter or ghee (clarified butter)
1 cup broken vermicelli or fine noodles
2 cups boiling water
1/2 cup mixed raisins and nuts (such as
   almonds or cashews), sprinkled with
   ground cinnamon and ground cardamom
1/2 cup sweetened condensed milk, heated

In a large saucepan over medium heat, melt the butter. Add the vermicelli and cook until lightly browned. Add the boiling water, increase the heat to high, and cook until the vermicelli is half done.

Add the raisin mixture and continue cooking until the vermicelli is soft. Drain off any excess water.

To serve, spoon the mixture into bowls and pour the milk over the top.

Yield: Makes 2 servings.

Mango-Fig Ice Cream

The much-beloved mango appears yet again, this time for dessert. Most Trinis recommend the Julie variety of mango. It is a small, tasty mango preferred because its pulp is not stringy. Don't be misled by the term "fig"; in this case, it refers to the tiny fig bananas.

1 cup evaporated milk
1 egg, beaten
1/2 cup mango pulp, sieved and chilled
1/2 cup mashed banana, preferably small
  fig bananas
2 cups whole milk
1/2 cup sugar
1/4 teaspoon freshly squeezed lime juice
Orange food coloring (optional)

In a large saucepan over low heat, combine the evaporated milk and the egg; cook to make a thin custard. Remove from the heat and let cool.

Add the mango, banana, whole milk, sugar, lime juice, and food coloring (if used); mix well. Transfer to an ice cream freezer and process according to the manufacturer's instructions. Serve chilled.

Yield: Makes 8 servings.

Coconut-Rice Pudding

It's only natural that two of T&T's most popular foods should be combined in a dessert. Cooks should feel free to add fruits such as raisins to this easy, semisweet treat.

2 cups cooked rice
1 cup coconut milk (page 36)
1/4 cup sugar
1/2 teaspoon ground allspice
1/2 teaspoon ground cinnamon
1/4 cup chopped nuts, such as almonds or
  pine nuts
1/2 teaspoon vanilla extract
Sliced bananas, for garnish

In a large saucepan over low heat, combine the rice, coconut milk, sugar, allspice, cinnamon, nuts, and vanilla. Cook, stirring occasionally, until the mixture thickens (about 5 minutes). Remove from the heat and serve either warm or cold, topped with sliced bananas.

Yield: Makes 4 servings.

Bananas in Rum Flambé

Serve this dessert outdoors in the evening, when the flaming bananas are the most spectacular. Variations of this dish are served all over the Caribbean, using all members of the *Musa* genus, from plantains to small fig bananas.

1/2 cup firmly packed brown sugar
2 tablespoons freshly squeezed lime juice
4 tablespoons butter
1/2 teaspoon ground cinnamon
1/2 teaspoon ground allspice
3 bananas, peeled and sliced in half lengthwise
1/4 cup light rum
1/4 cup coffee-flavored liqueur
Vanilla ice cream, for accompaniment

In a large skillet over medium heat, combine the brown sugar, lime juice, butter, cinnamon, and allspice. Cook until thick, stirring often. Add the bananas and cook until soft and well coated (about 4 minutes). Add the rum and liqueur and cook for 1 minute.

Ignite the contents of the skillet with a match, remove from the heat, and let the fire burn out. Remove the match if it fell into the skillet. Serve bananas covered with sauce and accompanied by ice cream.

Yield: Makes 6 servings.

Double Chocolate Mousse

Thanks to Joe Brown of the Solimar Restaurant for this creation. Yes, this dessert is sinful. Yes, this dessert should be reserved for a special splurge. Go for it! Note that it must be chilled for at least two hours before serving.

8 ounces (1 cup) semisweet chocolate
  couverture (see Note)
8 ounces (1 cup) white chocolate couverture
  (see Note)
2 tablespoons milk
6 egg whites
4 cups whipping cream
1 tablespoon white crème de cacao
1 tablespoon dark crème de cacao

In two small double boilers, melt the semisweet and white chocolate over simmering water, adding 1 tablespoon of milk to each to thin slightly. Stir until smooth, then allow to cool.

In a large chilled bowl, whip the egg whites until peaks form. In another large chilled bowl, whip the cream. Divide the whipped cream into 2 smaller bowls. Into one fold in the cooled melted white chocolate and white crème de cacao, then fold in half the egg whites. Set aside.

Into the second bowl of whipped cream, fold in the cooled melted semisweet chocolate and dark crème de cacao. Fold in the remaining egg whites.

Alternating layers, carefully spoon each mixture into tall parfait glasses. Chill for a minimum of 2 hours before serving.

Yield: Makes 6 to 8 servings, depending on the size of the glasses.

Note: Couverture is professional-quality cooking chocolate (minimum 32 percent cocoa butter), which is available at candy-making shops and some gourmet shops.

Trini Tropical Trifle

The European influence on T&T cookery is evident in this dessert. It's an English favorite usually made in the islands with canned fruit cocktail—which is ironic, considering the wealth of tropical fruits available. So we have taken the liberty of adapting the T&T version to reflect the tropical fruits of the country. This is a fairly complicated—but fun—recipe.

Sponge Cake

3 eggs
1 cup sugar
1 cup flour
1 teaspoon baking powder
1 tablespoon milk, heated
1 teaspoon grated orange zest

Fruit Filling

1 cup diced mangoes
1 cup diced pineapple
1 cup diced banana
1/4 cup sugar syrup, such as karo

Custard

6 egg yolks, slightly beaten
1/4 cup sugar
2 cups milk
1/2 teaspoon vanilla extract

Trifle

1/2 cup sherry
2 tablespoons rum
2 cups whipping cream, whipped until
  peaks form
1 cup fresh cherries, pitted and halved
1/2 cup slivered almonds

To make the cake, in a large bowl beat the eggs for 10 minutes, then gradually add the sugar. Fold in the flour, then add the baking powder, milk, and zest; mix well. Pour into a greased 9- by 5- by 3-inch baking pan and bake in a 350 degree F oven until a cake tester comes out clean (about 25 minutes). Remove from the oven and allow to cool.

To make the fruit filling, combine all of the ingredients in a large bowl.

To make the custard, place all of the ingredients in the top of a double boiler over hot water. Cook over low heat, stirring constantly, until the mixture coats a spoon (about 7 minutes). Remove from the heat and let cool in the refrigerator.

To assemble the trifle, cut the cake into 1-inch cubes and place in a shallow bowl. Combine the sherry and rum and pour over the cake cubes. Let stand until all the liquid has been absorbed.

Spread a thin layer of chilled custard over the bottom of a deep glass dish. Distribute the cake cubes uniformly over the custard, then spread the fruit filling evenly over all. Spread the remaining custard over the fruit, then spread the whipped cream over the top. Decorate with cherries and sprinkle with almonds. Refrigerate for at least 30 minutes before serving.

Yield: Makes 1 cake, 3 cups fruit filling, and 3 1/2 cups custard; serves 8.

T&T Orange-Iced Fudge Cake

There are probably hundreds of variations of chocolate cakes baked in T&T kitchens. We like the simplicity and intensity of this one, which is flavored with island oranges and cashews.

4 tablespoons butter
1 1/2 cups sugar
2 eggs, separated
4 ounces unsweetened chocolated, melted
2 tablespoons grated orange zest
1 3/4 cups cake flour
1 tablespoon baking powder
1/2 teaspoon salt
1 1/2 cups milk
1 teaspoon vanilla extract
1 cup chopped unsalted cashews

In a large bowl, cream together the butter and 1 1/4 cups of the sugar.

In a medium bowl, beat the egg yolks; add the chocolate and zest. Add the chocolate mixture to the butter mixture and combine thoroughly.

In another medium bowl, sift together the flour, baking powder, and salt; add to the chocolate-butter mixture alternately with milk. Beat until smooth. Add the vanilla and cashews and mix well.

Beat the egg whites until stiff; add the remaining 1/4 cup sugar and beat until very stiff. Fold the egg white mixture into the batter. Pour into 2 greased and floured 9-inch layer cake pans. Bake in a 350 degree F oven until a cake tester comes out clean (30 to 35 minutes). Remove from the oven and let cool on a wire rack.

Prepare the icing. Spread between the cooled cake layers, then ice the cake completely and serve.

Yield: Makes 6 to 8 servings.

Orange Icing
3 cups sugar
4 egg whites
2 teaspoons grated orange zest
2/3 cup orange juice

Combine all of the ingredients in the top of a double boiler over rapidly boiling water. Beat constantly with a whisk for 7 to 9 minutes, then remove from the heat. Continue beating until the icing is thick enough to spread.

Yield: Makes 2 cups.

Key Lime Cake

Here's a twist on Key lime pie. As the mixture bakes, the cake forms a light sponge layer with a delicious, rich sauce below it. It can be served warm or chilled with ice cream or whipped cream on top.

3 tablespoons butter or margarine
1 cup sugar
1/4 cup flour
3 eggs, separated
2 teaspoons grated lime zest
1/4 cup freshly squeezed lime juice,
   preferably from Key limes
1 1/2 cups milk
1/4 teaspoon salt

In a large bowl cream together the butter, 1/2 cup of the sugar, and flour. Add the egg yolks and beat well. Stir in the zest, lime juice, and milk. Set aside. Add the salt to the egg whites and beat until stiff. Gradually beat in the remaining 1/2 cup sugar. Fold into the butter mixture.

Pour the batter into a 1 1/2-quart buttered baking dish and set the dish in a large shallow pan containing boiling water to a depth of 1 inch. Bake in a 325 degree F oven for 1 hour. Allow to cool before serving.

Yield: Makes 6 servings.

Trinidad Black Cake

The only drawback to making Marie Permenter's version of the famous Trinidad black cake is that you have to start two months ahead of time! But it's worth the trouble—the final result is an incredibly rich, fruity, alcoholic cake. One small piece is enough to satisfy even the most decadent sweet tooth. We know from experience. These cakes are usually not frosted, but if they are served at Christmas, they can be topped with any frosting and decorated with colored fruits.

Step 1

1 pound seedless raisins
1 pound pitted prunes
1 pound dried currants
26 ounces dark rum
26 ounces cherry brandy or cherry wine
2 teaspoons vanilla extract
2 teaspoons almond extract
1 teaspoon ground allspice
1 teaspoon ground nutmeg
1 teaspoon ground cinnamon

Step 2

1/4 cup granulated sugar
1/4 cup boiling water
1 pound unsalted butter
1 pound brown sugar
1/2 pound mixed candied citrus peel
1/2 pound chopped nuts, such as walnuts
  or pecans
1 small bottle maraschino cherries, halved,
  juice reserved
1/4 cup glazed cherries, quartered
12 eggs
2 teaspoons grated lemon zest
4 cups flour
2 teaspoons baking powder
2 teaspoons baking soda
Rum or cherry brandy, if needed

Step 1

Combine all of the ingredients in a large crock or bowl, stir well, and cover. Let stand for 1 month in a cool place, stirring once a week.

Step 2

In a large saucepan over low heat, melt the granulated sugar and cook, stirring constantly, until golden brown. Stir in the boiling water; let cool. The syrup should be thick and dark brown.

In a large bowl cream together the butter and brown sugar. Add the soaked fruits from Step 1 and beat with a spoon. Add the mixed peel, nuts, maraschino cherries, and glazed cherries and continue beating.

Beat the eggs with lemon zest and fold into the fruit mixture.

Sift together the flour, baking powder, and baking soda; fold into the fruit mixture. Add 1 teaspoon each of the reserved cherry juice and cooled syrup; mix well. If the batter seems too thick, add a little rum or cherry brandy.

Line three 9-inch springform pans, or three 5 1/2- by 9-inch glass loaf pans, with waxed paper. (Pans should be as deep as possible.) Spread a light film of butter over the waxed paper. Pour in the batter, leaving 1 inch at the top of each pan. Bake in a 375 degree F oven for 1 hour, then reduce the heat to 150 degrees F and bake until a cake tester comes out clean (about 2 hours more). Let the cakes cool in the pans—do not remove them from the pans. When cool, wrap the cakes in the pans tightly in aluminum foil and store in a cool place for 1 month before serving.

Yield: Makes 3 cakes.

Note: At the bottom of the oven, place a cookie sheet full of water. It will add moisture, as well as catch any overflow from the cakes.

Orange-Chocolate Terrine

The combination of citrus and chocolate makes this elegant and calorie-laden dessert a treat for special occasions when you want to impress guests. The joy is that you can make it the day before. (Note that it must chill for three to four hours, or overnight.) We strongly recommend that you use only truly farm-fresh eggs to avoid any potential problems with salmonella. We've made this dessert several times with no adverse effects—except for gaining weight. Thanks to Joe Brown of the Solimar Restaurant for this recipe.

Step 1

4 oranges, zest reserved and minced
1 1/2 cups sugar
4 eggs, separated
1/2 teaspoon freshly squeezed lemon juice
1/8 teaspoon salt
2 cups whipping cream

Step 2

6 ounces bittersweet chocolate
1/2 cup plus 2 tablespoons sugar
6 eggs, separated
1/8 teaspoon salt
2 cups whipping cream
Semisweet chocolate curls, for garnish

Step 1

Squeeze the oranges, strain the juice, and place in a heavy saucepan. Combine the zest with 1/2 cup of the sugar; add to the juice and bring to a boil, then cook over medium-high heat until mixture becomes a heavy syrup. Remove from the heat and let cool until warm.

Beat the egg yolks, then slowly pour in the warm syrup in a ribbon.

Whip the egg whites with the remaining 1 cup sugar, lemon juice, and salt until soft peaks form. Set aside.

Whip the cream. Combine it with the egg-orange mixture and the egg white mixture, stirring gently. Spread the mixture in a 9- by 13-inch glass baking dish. Refrigerate for about 1 hour.

Step 2

Melt the chocolate in a double boiler over simmering water; add the sugar and cook slowly until the sugar is melted. Remove from the heat and add the egg yolks, stirring briskly until they are well blended. Let the mixture cool slightly.

Add the salt to the egg whites and beat until stiff peaks form. Set aside.

Whip the cream; gently fold in the chocolate mixture and the beaten egg whites. Spread over the chilled orange mixture, then refrigerate until firm (3 to 4 hours, or overnight).

To serve, cut the terrine into squares and turn out carefully with a spatula. No additional whipped cream topping is necessary. Garnish with chocolate curls.

Yield: Makes 10 to 12 servings.

Appendix

Glossary of T&T Terms

We have endeavored to be as accurate as possible in this compilation, but because of the ethnic mix of people in T&T, spellings and definitions often vary considerably.

Accra. Highly seasoned fritter usually made with salted fish.

Agouti. Edible, rabbitlike rodent.

Allspice (*Pimenta dioica*). The words *pimenta* or *pimento* apply to this nutmeg-tasting island spice, not to *Capsicum* pepper, which is the pimiento used to stuff olives.

Aloo. Potatoes.

Amchar. Mango; also a type of *masala* used to season cooked green mangoes.

Anchaar. Hot East Indian curried pickle, often made with sun-dried mangoes. Also spelled *amchar* and *anchar*.

Bacalao. Salt cod.

Bake. Native bread that is either fried or baked.

Balangen. *Melongene*, eggplant.

Beigun. Eggplant.

Bellyfull. Any filling food. Also, a type of dessert.

Black pudding. Blood sausage.

Bodi. String beans more than a yard long.

Boucanee. Process of smoking with fire and wet leaves.

Breadfruit (*Artocarpus communis*). Round green fruit available fresh and canned in the United States. The weight of the fresh fruit varies from 2 to 5 pounds.

Buljol. Dish made with salted fish and seasoned with lime, tomatoes, and onions.

Bun-bun. Burned layer on bottom of *pelau* pan.

Bush. Anything green and leafy.

Bush meat. Game such as iguana, agouti, opossum, or armadillo.

Buss-up-shut. Flaky bread served with curries. The name derives from "burst-up-shirt," a reference to the torn-cloth appearance of the bread.

Callaloo. Green leaves of the aroid *Colocasia esculenta*, or taro; also, soup or stew made with those leaves.

Cascadura. Primitive, oily, armored catfish that is an island delicacy.

Cassareep. Boiled-down cassava juice.

Cassava (*Manihot esculenta*). Edible root also called manioc, yuca, and tapioca, which must be cooked before being eaten. It is available fresh, frozen, and canned in the United States. All the peel, both ends, and stringy fiber in the center must be removed before eating.

Chadon bene. See Shadow Bennie.

Channa. Chick-peas or garbanzo beans.

Chip-chip. Edible mollusk found at low tide on the beach. Also, a Trinidadian coconut candy. Also, a dance step.

Christophene. Chayote (*Sechium edule*), a type of squash.

Chutney. East Indian condiment, sometimes hot and spicy and sometimes sweet. The Hindi word is *chatni*, sometimes *chutni*.

Congo. Local name for the T&T pod type of *Capsicum chinense*, a hot pepper species called Habanero in Mexico and Scotch bonnet in Jamaica.

Coo-coo. Okra and cornmeal "bread."

Cush-cush. Yam.

Dasheen. Leaves of the taro plant.

Dhal. Split peas, sometimes spelled *dal*.

Doubles. Curried *channa* served between two pieces of fried bread.

Figs. Small bananas.

Floats. Fried yeast bread.

Funity. Bundle of soup ingredients, such as turnips, carrots, celery, and thyme.

Granadilla. Passion fruit.

Ground provisions. Root crops, such as taro, carrots, and potatoes.

Hops bread. Baked yeast bread.

Jeera. Cumin, also spelled *jira*.

Jelly nut. Soft, unformed flesh of an immature coconut, considered a delicacy.

Jumbie. Zombie.

Kucheela. Hot and spicy East Indian mango relish, also spelled *kuchela* and *kuchila*.

Kurma. East Indian candy made from deep-fried flour, then coated with sugar.

Lambie. Conch.

Lappe. Rabbit.

Makaforshet. Leftovers.

Manicou. Opossum.

Masala. Spice blend used in curry dishes.

Mauby. Bark of the Caribbean carob tree *Colubrina reclinata* used to make a drink of the same name. The dried bark is often sold in Latin markets in the United States.

Melongene. Eggplant.

Ochro. Okra.

Oil-down. To cook absorbent fruits and vegetables in coconut milk until milk is absorbed, leaving only a film of coconut oil in pan.

Pachro. Sea urchin.

Pan. Steel drum.

Passion fruit. Tasty fruit of the tropical vine *Passiflora edulis*.

Pawpaw. Papaya.

Pelau. Native rice dish of meat, peas, and coconut milk.

Phulouri. Fried split-pea appetizer.

Pigeon pea (*Cajanus cajun*). Similar to black-eyed pea. Also called *gandule* or *gungo*.

Piri piri. Hot and spicy Portuguese pepper oil.

Plantain (*Musa paradisica*). Long banana-like fruit used both green and ripe. When green, they are fried, added to stews, and made into dumplings. When ripe, they are fried, eaten as a vegetable, added to breads, and made into desserts.

Poncha crema. Trinidadian eggnog.

Pumpkin (*Cucurbita moschata*). Technically, this is a winter squash rather than what is known as a pumpkin in the United States. The hard skin is normally orange. Hubbard, acorn, or butternut squash can be substituted.

Quenk. Wild pig; peccary.

Roocoo. Achiote; annatto seeds.

Roti. Curried filling wrapped in *chapati* bread. Also, various breads used to make *roti*.

Saffron (or Indian saffron). Turmeric.

Saheena. Fritter made with ground *channa* and *dasheen* leaves. Also spelled *sahina*.

Salt cod. Salted fish, which must be soaked in water and rinsed several times before using. Any cooked white fish is an acceptable substitute.

Sancoche. A filling T&T stew.

Sea moss. Gelatinous drink made from dried kelp.

Sewain. Vermicelli dessert popular at Muslim festivals. Also spelled *sawine*.

Shaddock (*Citrus grandis*). Grapefruit-like fruit, also called pomelo.

Shadow Bennie. Nickname for *chadon bene*, an aromatic herb (*Eryngium foetidum*) used in sauces and stews. The Spanish name is *culantro*; the Hindi name is *bandhania*.

Sorrel. Sepals of a species of hibiscus, used to make a drink.

Souse. Popular Sunday breakfast dish made from pickled pork.

Talkaree. Vegetables cooked down as an accompaniment to rice or *roti*. Also spelled *talkari*.

Tamarind (*Tanarindus indicus*). Bean-bearing tree brought to the West Indies from India. Pods are used fresh and dried. Fresh pulp surrounding seeds is extracted and sold as fruit nectar and pulp in Latin and Asian markets. Seeds, surrounded with dried pulp, can be scraped out of dried pods and rehydrated.

Tannia (*Xanthosoma sagittifolium*). Root vegetable called by a number of names, including yellow *malanga*. Commonly served in soups and stews.

Taro (*Colocasia esculenta*). Edible tuber rich in starch. Also called eddo.

Tatoo. Armadillo.

Tawa. Large, flat griddle for cooking *roti* breads.

Taza sale. Salted kingfish.

Toolum. Sticky candy made from molasses and grated coconut. Also spelled *tulum*.

Tum-tum. Mashed green plantain.

Yam (*Dioscorea batatas*). Favorite T&T tuber. Sweet potato may be substituted.

Yuca. Cassava.

Zaboca. Avocado.

T&T Resources

Tourism Information

T&T Tourism Development Authority
134-138 Frederick Street, P.O. Box 122
Port of Spain
Trinidad & Tobago, W.I.
(809) 623-1932
FAX (809) 623-3848

Ask for their excellent publication *Discover Trinidad & Tobago*.

T&T Tourism Development Authority
25 W. 43rd Street, Ste. 1508
New York, NY 10036
(800) 232-0082
(212) 719-0540
FAX (212) 719-0988

This office provides a list of current hotel and guest room rates.

General Information

Location and population. The islands are the southernmost in the Caribbean and are just off the coast of Venezuela. There are about 1.3 million people in T&T, of African, Portuguese, East Indian, Chinese, Spanish, Lebanese, French, and English descent.

Climate. The average temperature is 83 degrees F. June through December is the wet season, with brief downpours for a few hours a day.

Language. English. Some Hindi is spoken.

Money. The Trinidad and Tobago dollar (TT$) floats around 5.768 to one U.S. dollar. U.S. dollars are not officially accepted, but on occasion merchants will request them. It's best to change money at the airport or a bank as soon as you arrive. All major credit cards are accepted throughout the country. A departure tax of TT$75 is charged. These figures are subject to change.

Telephones. Telephones and fax machines are ubiquitous and function well. The area code is 809, which can be direct-dialed from the United States.

Electricity. The standard is 115 volts AC, so American appliances work fine without converters.

Passports. All visitors must have a valid passport. Visas are not needed for visitors from the United States, the United Kingdom, and most European countries. Contact the Tourism Development Authority for more information.

Airlines Serving T&T

BWIA from Miami, New York, Toronto, and Europe
Aeropostal from Caracas
Air Canada from Toronto
American from San Juan, Puerto Rico and from Miami
British Airways from London
KLM from Amsterdam
LIAT from other Caribbean islands
United from New York and Caracas

Tour Guides

For such tours as turtle watching at Matura Bay, the Caroni Bird Sanctuary, beach tours, religious festivals, and fishing trips, the following tour guides are available in 1993.

Travel Trinidad & Tobago
69 Independence Square
Port of Spain
Trinidad & Tobago, W.I.
(809) 625-2201

TNT Explorers
Royal Palm Plaza
7 Saddle Road, Maraval
Port of Spain
Trinidad & Tobago, W.I.
(809) 628-7481

Hibiscus Tours
22 10th Avenue
Bataravia
Trinidad & Tobago, W.I.
(809) 675-2537

T&T Hospitality Services
61 Picton Street, Newtown
Port of Spain
Trinidad & Tobago, W.I.
(809) 628-1051

Bayshore Charters
29 Sunset Drive
Bayshore
Trinidad & Tobago, W.I.
(809) 637-8711

Mail Order Sources for Hot Sauces and Other Caribbean Ingredients

Cardullo's Gourmet Shop
6 Brattle Street
Cambridge, MA 02138

Caribbean Food Products, Inc.
1936 N. Second Avenue
Jacksonville Beach, FL 32250
(904) 246-0149
FAX (904) 246-7273

The Central Grocery
923 Decatur Street
New Orleans, LA 70166

Cottage Industries
201 Saddle Hills Road
Burleson, TX 76028

Creole Marketplace
885-887 Nostrand Avenue
Brooklyn, NY 10014

Dean and DeLuca
560 Broadway
New York, NY 10012

Delmar Imports
501 Monroe Street
Detroit, MI 48226

Frieda's by Mail
P.O. Box 58488
Los Angeles, CA 90058
(800) 241-1771

La Tienda Specialty Foods
190 Boggs Avenue
Virginia Beach, VA 23462

Old Southwest Trading Co.
P.O. Box 7545
Albuquerque, NM 87194

Spectacular Sauces
P.O. Box 30010
Alexandria, VA 22310

Mail Order Sources for Calypso, Soca, and Steel Band Music

Afri-Caribe Records
6832 New Hampshire Drive
Tacoma Park, MD 20912
(301) 270-0827

Rankin Records
164 N.E. 167th Street
North Miami, FL 33162
(305) 940-2510

Bibliography

For food, music, and travel aficionados, here are some suggestions for additional information on the culture of T&T.

Ahye, Molly
1987. "Caribbean Carnival." In *Trinidad & Tobago. An Insight Guide.* Singapore: APA Productions.

Anon
1956. "Sounds from the Caribbean." *Time*, Vol. 67, Feb. 27, 47.
1957. "The Calypso Craze." *Newsweek*, Feb. 25, 72.
1957. "Calypsomania." *Time*, Vol. 69, Mar. 25, 55.

Anthony, Michael and Andrew Carr, eds.
1975. *David Frost Introduces Trinidad & Tobago.* London: Andre Deutsch.

Baptiste, Rhona
1992. *Dialect by Day: 365 Trini Words* (calendar). Port of Spain: Inprint Caribbean Ltd.

Barrow, Errol W. and Kendall A. Lee
1988. *Privilege: Cooking in the Caribbean.* London: Macmillan Caribbean.

Bastyra, Judy
1987. *Caribbean Cooking.* Kingston, Jamaica: Heinemann Publishers (Caribbean).

Bourne, M. J., et al.
1988. *Fruits and Vegetables of the Caribbean.* London: Macmillan Caribbean.

Brown, Ernest
1987. "Musical Nation." In *Trinidad & Tobago. An Insight Guide*. Singapore: APA Productions.

Brown, Les
1956. "The Mighty Panther Tells Roots, Meanings of Calypso." *Down Beat*, Vol. 23, May 30, 42.

Carr, Andrew
1975. "Carnival." In *David Frost Introduces Trinidad and Tobago*. London: Andre Deutsch.

Castagne, Patrick S.
1958. "This is Calypso." *Music Journal*, Jan., 32.

Clark, E. Phyllis
1945. *West Indian Cookery*. Edinburgh, Scotland: Thomas Nelson & Sons.

Crowley, Daniel J.
1959. "Toward a Definition of Calypso." *Ethnomusicology*, Vol. 3, No. 2 (May), 57.

De Boissiere, Jean
1948. *Cooking Creole: Suggestions on Making Creole Food*. Second edition, 1992, ed. by Gerard Besson. Port of Spain: Paria Publishing.

DeWitt, Dave and Mary Jane Wilan
1993. "Down de Islands." *Chile Pepper*, Jan./Feb.

Editors of Rolling Stone
1983. *Rolling Stone Rock Almanac*. New York: Macmillan.

Eliot, Ann
1957. "Real, Real Calypso." *Dance Magazine*, Vol. 31, July and Oct., 30 and 36.

Ganase, Pat
1992. "Lord of the Dance." *BWee Caribbean Beat*, No. 3 (Autumn), 4.

Hector, Richard
1992. "Soca Busting Out All Over." *Port of Spain Sunday Express Living*, Aug. 9, 20.

Hill, Errol
1967. "On the Origin of the Term Calypso," *Ethnomusicology*, Vol. XI, No. 3 (Sept.), 359.

1972. *The Trinidad Carnival: Mandate for a National Theatre*. Austin: University of Texas Press.

Holder, Geoffrey
1955. "Drumming on Steel Barrel-Heads." *Music Journal*, May-June, 9.

1957. "That Fad from Trinidad." *New York Times Magazine*, April 21, 14.

Hunt, Sylvia
1985. *Sylvia Hunt's Cooking*. Port of Spain: Scrip-J Printers.

1985. *Sylvia Hunt's Sweets*. Port of Spain: Scrip-J Printers.

Indar, Polly B., et al., eds.
1988. *Naparima Girls' High School Diamond Jubilee (1912-1987) Recipe Book*. San Fernando, T&T: Naparima Girls' High School.

Mackie, Christine
1992. *Life and Food in the Caribbean*. New York: New Amsterdam Books.

Mahabir, Kumar
1991. *Medicinal and Edible Plants Used by East Indians of Trinidad and Tobago*. El Dorado, T&T: Chakra Publishing House.

McLane, Daisann
1981. "Why Calypso When You Can Soca?" *Village Voice*, Vol. 26, Sept. 2, 56.

1984. "Riffs: Making History." *Village Voice*, Vol. 29, Sept. 11, 65.

1989. "High Mas." *Caribbean Travel and Life*, Jan./Feb., 63.

1989. "Road Warriors." *Village Voice*, Vol. 34, Mar. 7, 76.

1991. "Trinidad on the Hudson." *The New York Times Magazine*, Jan. 6, 37.

Moses, Knolly
1987. "Roti on the Run." In *Trinidad & Tobago. An Insight Guide*. Singapore: APA Productions.

Naipaul, Shiva
1973. *The Chip-Chip Gatherers*. New York: Penguin.

Nelson, Kay Shaw
1992. "Cooking Callaloo." *Caribbean Travel and Life*, Nov./Dec., 92.

Nizer, Louis
1961. *My Life in Court*. New York: Doubleday.

Ortiz, Elisabeth Lambert
1973. *The Complete Book of Caribbean Cooking*. New York: M. Evans.

Pitt, Yvonne and Vilma Bier
1985. *Our Own Cookbook of Trinidad and Tobago and Brazil*. Port of Spain: The College Press.

Saft, Elizabeth, ed.
1987. *Trinidad & Tobago. An Insight Guide*. Singapore: APA Productions.

Sahni, Julie
1992. "Curry Power." *Caribbean Travel and Life*, Mar./April, 72.

Shaw, Arnold
1960. *Belafonte: An Unauthorized Biography*. New York: Chilton Company.

Simon, Pete
1975. "Steelband." In *David Frost Introduces Trinidad and Tobago*. London: Andre Deutsch.

Smith, Keith, ed. c.
1987. *Sparrow the Legend*. Port of Spain: Inprint Caribbean Ltd.

Sokolov, Raymond
1991. "A Portable Feast." (*Rotis*). *Natural History*, May, 84.

Subramanian, Aruna
1988. *Aruna's Vegetarian Recipes*. Port of Spain: Indian Women's Group of Trinidad and Tobago.

Taylor, Jeremy, ed.
1992. *Discover Trinidad and Tobago*. Port of Spain: MEP.

Warner, Keith
1983. *Kaiso: The Trinidad Calypso*. London: Heinemann.

Discography

The listings below are by no means complete, because calypso and *soca* recording artists appear on many hard-to-find local labels throughout the Caribbean and the United States. But here are some of our favorite calypso, steel band, and *soca* recordings, which are fairly accessible in the States. The format is compact disk (CD) unless otherwise indicated. Look for these and other titles at Third World and specialty record stores, Caribbean shops, Caribbean airport gift shops, and in or near the reggae and Latin music bins in the large record chain stores. Search used record shops as well, especially for titles in vinyl format.

Arrow (Alphonsus Cassell)
1988. *Knock Dem Dead*. New York: Mango (Island), CCD 9809.
1989. *O'La Soca*. New York: Mango (Island), CCD 9835.
1990. *Soca Dance Party*. New York: Mango/Antilles, MAN9878

Black Stalin (Leroy Calliste)
1986. *Sing for the Land*. Brooklyn: B's Records, BSR-BS-053. (Vinyl.)

Mighty Sparrow (Slinger Francisco)
1989. *Party Classics*. St. Thomas, V.I.: Gutu Corp., PF1948 49 CD.
1992. *Sparrow vs. The Rest*. New York: Discos CBS International, DiS80441.

Our Boys Steel Orchestra
1991. *Pan Progress*. New York: Island Records, 162 539 916-2.

Rudder, David
1990. *1990*. New York: Sire Records, 26250-2.

Rudder, David and Charlie's Roots
1988. *Haiti*. New York: Sire Records, 25723-2.

Tambu (Chris Herbert) and Charlie's Roots
1987. *Culture*. New York: Sire Records, 25741-2.

Various Artists

N.D. *Steel Band Music of the Caribbean*. Legacy International, CD 307.
1986. *This Is Soca*, 2. (Mighty Grynner, Arrow, Charlie's Roots). London Records, LP 828 0171. (Vinyl)
1989. *Calypso Pioneers*, 1912-37. Rounder, RoU1039. (Attila the Hun, Wilmoth Houdini, et al.)
1990. *Calypso Breakaway*, 1927-41. Rounder, RoU1054. (Attila the Hun, Lion, Tiger, et al.)
1990. *Calypso Season*. New York: Mango/Antilles, MAN9861.
1992. *Calypsos from Trinidad: Politics, Intrigue and Violence I*. Arhoolie, ARH7004.
1992. *The Best of Rootsman and Bally*. Brooklyn: J.W. Records, JWCD-1005.
1992. *CD Compilation* (Explainer, Designer, Bally). Brooklyn: J.W. Records, JWCD-1006.

Index

Notes

Notes

Notes